Theme-A-Saur
Dinosaurs

Ages 3–6

By Marsha Elyn Wright

Published by Totline® Publications
an imprint of

Children's Publishing

Author: Marsha Elyn Wright
Editor: Karen Thompson

 **Children's Publishing**

Published by Totline® Publications
An imprint of McGraw-Hill Children's Publishing
Copyright © 2004 McGraw-Hill Children's Publishing

Send all inquiries to:
McGraw-Hill Children's Publishing
3195 Wilson Drive NW
Grand Rapids, Michigan 49544

Theme-a-Saurus: Dinosaurs—PreK–K
ISBN: 1-57029-483-6

1 2 3 4 5 6 7 8 9 MAL 09 08 07 06 05 04

Table of Contents

Reproducible Dinosaur Incentives

Introduction

Invite children to explore the amazing wonders of the dinosaur kingdom. *Dinosaurs* is designed to be used as a springboard and resource for both teachers and parents of young children. This valuable teaching resource is packed with meaningful activities that promote creativity, curiosity, and self-confidence in young learners. The open-ended, no-lose ideas are categorized into major curriculum areas for easy access.

Dinosaurs offers imaginative ways for children to develop such basic skills as observing, measuring, predicting, experimenting, counting, prereading, and prewriting. The variety of ideas and activities immerse children in learning situations that allow them to freely experiment without the fear of failure. It also helps children develop the skills they need to be successful in school, such as visual discrimination, one-to-one correspondence, oral expression, fine and gross motor movement, and dramatic play.

As with all *Theme-A-Saurus* books, *Dinosaurs* offers a myriad of hands-on opportunities for children to acquire basic as well as critical and creative thinking skills through meaningful activities that inspire their imaginations! Invite children to join you as you share the awesome world of dinosaurs!

The following creative and visual experiences give young children opportunities to express themselves and communicate their ideas and feelings through art.

Art

Tissue Paper Skin and Scales

Materials:

- large sheet of butcher paper
- Styrofoam trays
- white glue
- water
- different colored tissue paper
- scissors

To prepare for the activity, cut the butcher paper into a wall-sized dinosaur shape. Cut the tissue paper into squares. Mix water and glue in trays. Invite children to name the dinosaur. Let children dip squares of tissue paper into the glue mix and use them to add wild colors of "skin and scales" on the dinosaur.

Shoe Polish Habitats

Materials:

- plastic bottles of white, black, and brown liquid shoe polish, with sponge applicators
- food coloring
- blue and green construction paper
- scissors

Cut small dinosaur shapes from green paper, two for each child. Pry the sponge applicator tops off the bottles of white polish, and add drops of food coloring to make different colors. Give each child a sheet of blue paper and two dinosaur shapes. Have children glue their dinosaurs on their paper. Demonstrate how to use the applicator like a giant marker and draw trees, bushes, ferns, rocks, and lakes on the paper. Hang the artwork on a clothesline strung across the room. Add the title "Hung Up on Habitats."

Dinosaur Tracks

Materials:

- white construction paper
- inkpads
- paper towels
- crayons or markers

Show children pictures of dinosaurs in their habitats of long ago. Have each child draw a prehistoric environment with trees, lakes, grass, rocks, hills, and volcanoes. Let children press their fingertips on stamp pads and make dinosaur "footprints" in and around their habitats. Show children how to add claw marks on each print using a black crayons or markers. Invite children to take turns talking about their artwork.

Dinosaur Rubbings

Materials:

- cardboard
- tagboard
- construction paper, mesh or screen pieces
- peeled crayons
- scissors

Cut out a dinosaur pattern from tagboard; one pattern for each pair of children. Give each child a sheet of construction paper. Show how to trace the pattern on construction paper and cut it out. Have each child lay pieces of mesh or screen on cardboard and place his or her dinosaur on top of the mesh. Let children rub across their dinosaurs with the sides of crayons to make crisscross patterns. Tell children to press down hard while coloring.

Marbleized Prehistoric Pictures

Materials:

- black and white construction paper
- pie tins
- plastic dishes
- marbles (two per child)
- two or three colors of thick tempera paint
- paint smocks

Have children wear paint smocks. Cut out small dinosaur shapes and fern-like trees from black construction paper, so each child gets two dinosaurs and one tree. Cut white construction paper to fit in the bottom of the pie tins, one tin per child. Pour a small amount of paint into each plastic dish. Drop a marble into each color of paint and roll it around to coat the marble. Let children take turns carefully placing different marbles in his or her pie tin. Demonstrate how to roll a paint-coated marble back and forth across the paper. The marbles will leave a trail of colors, crisscrossing over each other. Let dry. Then have children arrange and glue their dinosaurs and trees on their marbleized prehistoric settings!

Torn Paper Creatures

Materials:

- different colored butcher paper
- black felt pens or crayons

Cover your wall from the floor up with blue paper. Tear brown tree trunks, fern-like green leaves, and white puffy clouds. Arrange these on the paper to create a prehistoric setting. Show children different-shaped dinosaurs (rounded, sharp-edged, long, tall). Invite children to create torn paper dinosaurs out of a variety of colors of butcher paper. Encourage them to add eyes, teeth, and other details with black pens or crayons. Let each child share his or her dinosaur before pinning it in the prehistoric picture.

Art

Shape Dinosaurs

Materials:

- different colored construction paper
- glue
- scissors

Cut simple geometric shapes—circles, squares, triangles, and rectangles—out of different colored paper. Give each child a sheet of green construction paper and a number of shapes in different colors and sizes. Let each child arrange and glue different shapes on the green paper to make an imaginative dinosaur creature. Invite children to talk about their creations.

Sponge-Print Bones

Materials:

- tagboard
- small sponge pieces
- paint
- meat trays
- paper towels
- scissors

Make stamp pads by placing folded paper towels in the trays and pouring small amounts of paint on the towels. Cut out different sizes and shapes of dinosaur bones from tagboard. Give each child a "bone." Let children dip sponge pieces in the paint and dab them on their bones. Cover a section of your classroom wall or a bulletin board with black paper. Let children help you arrange and pin their sponge-painted bones on the paper to create one imaginative dinosaur! You can make this creature your class mascot while you study dinosaurs!

Splatter-Paint Dinosaurs

Materials:

- wire screen pieces
- masking tape
- newspaper
- tempera paint
- shallow paint dishes
- old toothbrushes
- construction paper
- tagboard
- scissors

Cut out simple dinosaur stencils from tagboard, one per child. Cover the work area with newspaper. (Note: Fold masking tape along the edges of each screen for safety.) Have each child place a dinosaur stencil on top of a sheet of construction paper. Let each child hold a screen over his or her paper, dip a toothbrush into paint, and brush it on the screen so the paint splatters onto the paper. Show children how the area covered by the dinosaur stencil stays free from paint. Tell children to wash their toothbrushes, and then splatter a different colored paint onto their paper. Suggest to children that they can move their stencils before splattering on more paint. Let dry. Frame each picture by gluing it onto a larger sheet of construction paper in a contrasting color.

Contact Paper Dinosaurs

Materials:
- contact paper
- construction paper scraps
- wrapping paper
- scissors

For each child, cut a simple dinosaur shape (Apatosaurus or Stegosaurus) out of contact paper. Remove the backing from each shape. Cut the construction scraps and wrapping paper into small squares. Give each child a dinosaur shape. Have them place the shapes on the table in front of them, sticky side up. Tell children that scientists don't really know the true colors of dinosaurs. Demonstrate how to press paper pieces on the sticky surface to fill in the dinosaur shape. (You may want to cover the finished dinosaurs with clear plastic wrap, since uncovered areas of the adhesive surface will be sticky.) Let children share their creations with the class. Invite children to name their dinosaurs too!

Fruit Stamp Dinosaurs

Materials:
- tagboard
- tempera paint
- meat trays
- thin sponges or paper towels
- knife, fruits (e.g., apples, lemons, oranges)
- scissors

For each child, cut a simple dinosaur shape out of tagboard. Cut the fruits in cross sections to make flat printing surfaces. Put sponges or folded paper towels in trays, and pour different colors of tempera paint in each tray. Pair up children. Give each pair some fruit "stamps" and a paint tray. Give each child a dinosaur shape. Have children dip the fruits in paint and use them to stamp designs on their dinosaurs. Display the finished dinosaurs side by side on a wall, and add the title "Dinosaurs on Parade!"

Crumpled Paper Mural

Materials:
- brown grocery bags
- butcher paper
- black felt pens
- scissors

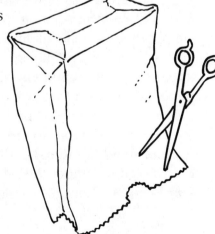

Cover a section of wall with blue butcher paper. Cut wide strips from green butcher paper, and cut slits along one edge to make "grass." Attach strips along the bottom of the wall. Cut each grocery bag so it lies flat, and give each child a bag. Show how to crumple a bag into a ball and flatten it again. Let children use black pens to draw a big dinosaur on the wrinkled paper. Invite children to draw triangular spikes along the top of their dinosaurs' bodies and tails, and add facial features. Ask adult helpers to cut out the dinosaurs; this part is difficult for children. Host a "Dino Day" when children can talk about their creatures.

Art

Gigantic Potato-Print Dinosaur

Materials:

- large sheet of brown butcher paper
- tempera paint
- meat trays
- thin sponges or paper towels
- knife
- potatoes
- scissors

Cut the butcher paper into a large dinosaur shape, and then cut the potatoes into various shapes. Place sponges or folded paper towels in the trays, and pour different colors of paint in each tray. Display the dinosaur on a wall. First, invite children to name the dinosaur. Then work together to write a class story about it. Finally, let children dip potato pieces in paint and make prints on the dinosaur until the entire shape is covered.

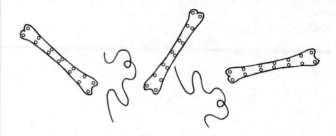

Lacing Dinosaur Bones

Materials:

- tagboard
- different colored yarn
- hole punch
- masking tape
- scissors

Cut out dinosaur bone shapes from tagboard. Punch holes around the edge of each bone, about one inch apart. Cut yarn into appropriate lengths for lacing around the bones. Wrap a piece of masking tape around one end of each length of yarn to form a "needle." Tape the other end of each yarn piece to the back of each bone. Give each child a bone. Let children lace yarn through the holes. When children are finished lacing, trim the yarn ends and tape them to the backs of the bones.

Dinosaur Zoo

Materials:

- paint smocks
- white construction paper
- glue
- different colored construction paper
- plastic berry baskets
- tempera paint
- shallow pie pans
- newspaper
- scissors

Have children wear paint smocks, and cover the work area with newspaper. Pour different colors of paint in separate pie pans. Cut out simple dinosaur shapes in different sizes and colors from construction paper. Let children arrange and glue different dinosaurs on white paper. Then have them dip the bottoms of plastic berry baskets in paint and press them over the white paper to create "fences" in front of the dinosaurs. Let dry. Display children's pictures under the title "Welcome to Our Dinosaur Zoo."

Paper Plate Dinosaurs

Materials:

- large paper plates
- construction paper
- glue
- tempera paint
- meat trays
- thin sponges or paper towels
- crayons
- knife
- vegetables such as carrots, onions, mushrooms, and cauliflower

Cut each paper plate in half to make two dinosaur bodies. (Make one dinosaur body for each child.) Cut construction paper circles for dinosaur heads and construction paper rectangles for dinosaur legs. Prepare one head and four legs for each dinosaur. Cut the vegetables in cross-sections to make flat printing surfaces and interesting shapes. Place sponges or folded paper towels in the trays, and pour different colors of tempera paint in each tray. Pair up children. Give each pair a set of vegetable "stamps" and a paint tray. Then give each child a dinosaur body, head, and four legs. Have children dip the vegetables in paint and use them to stamp designs on their dinosaur plates. Let dry. Demonstrate where to glue the head and legs on a dinosaur. Encourage children to use their crayons to draw eyes, mouths, and toes on their dinosaurs.

Bubble-Print Dinosaurs

Materials:

- black and white construction paper
- tempera paint, liquid detergent
- water
- quart container
- pie pans
- nonflexible straws
- thick black markers
- scissors

Twenty-four hours in advance, prepare equal portions of paint and liquid soap in a quart container. Add water and stir. To make different colors, prepare a separate mixture for each. Poke holes near the tops of the straws to prevent children from sucking up soapy paint. Cut out large squares of white construction paper. The day of the activity, pour different paint mixtures into separate pie pans. Let two children at a time blow bubbles with straws in each mixture. After bubbles are quite high, let each child take a turn slowly lowering a paper square onto the bubbles, being careful not to touch the water. The paint bubbles will pop, leaving interesting designs. (HINT: If the bubbles pop too quickly, add a few tablespoons of sugar to the water.) Let dry. Frame each bubble print by gluing it onto a larger square of black paper. Let children use thick black markers to draw dinosaurs on their bubble prints.

Art

Nature Print Prehistoric Pictures

Materials:

- green, red, and yellow tempera paint
- pie pans
- white construction paper
- black and other colored paper scraps
- paintbrush
- scissors
- crayons
- greenery (weeds, ferns, leaves)

Place a small amount of each color of paint in a separate pie pan. Mix different shades of green by adding yellow (you can make different shades of yellow by adding red). Give each child a white sheet of construction paper and some greenery. Demonstrate how to paint each leaf, one at a time, with different colors. Show how to carefully place the painted side of each piece of greenery on white paper; and then lay a piece of scrap paper over the top and gently press down. Encourage children to overlap their prints to create a lush prehistoric habitat. When they're finished, have them remove the leaves. While the paint is drying, let children draw imaginative dinosaurs on black paper and cut them out. Let children glue their dinosaurs on their habitats.

Handprint Plated Dinosaur Prints

Materials:

- paint smocks
- tempera paint
- construction paper
- paper towels
- waxed paper
- black markers

Have children wear paint smocks. Spread paint on sheets of waxed paper. Let children place their hands in paint and press them, paint side down, on construction paper. Tell them to move their fingers back and forth. (The palm becomes the dinosaur's body, the fingers become the plated back, and the thumb becomes the head.) After the paint dries, have children use markers to add facial features.

Sun-Print Fossils

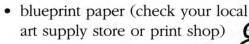

Materials:

- blueprint paper (check your local art supply store or print shop)
- cardboard
- variety of leaves
- small dinosaur stencils
- scissors

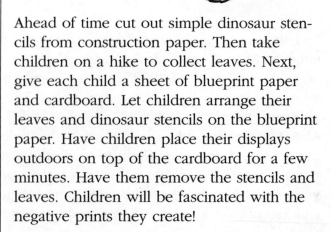

Ahead of time cut out simple dinosaur stencils from construction paper. Then take children on a hike to collect leaves. Next, give each child a sheet of blueprint paper and cardboard. Let children arrange their leaves and dinosaur stencils on the blueprint paper. Have children place their displays outdoors on top of the cardboard for a few minutes. Have them remove the stencils and leaves. Children will be fascinated with the negative prints they create!

Clay Dinosaurs

Materials:

- water-based clay
- waxed paper
- newspaper
- craft sticks
- screen or burlap scraps
- containers of water
- tempera paint
- paintbrushes
- shellac

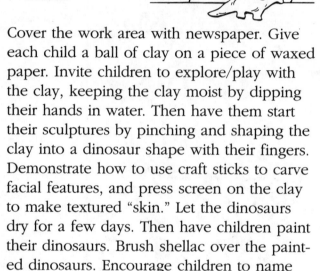

Cover the work area with newspaper. Give each child a ball of clay on a piece of waxed paper. Invite children to explore/play with the clay, keeping the clay moist by dipping their hands in water. Then have them start their sculptures by pinching and shaping the clay into a dinosaur shape with their fingers. Demonstrate how to use craft sticks to carve facial features, and press screen on the clay to make textured "skin." Let the dinosaurs dry for a few days. Then have children paint their dinosaurs. Brush shellac over the painted dinosaurs. Encourage children to name their creatures and share them with the class.

Crayon Transfers

Materials:

- white construction paper
- crayons
- light-colored chalk (different from crayon colors)
- pencils

Give each child two sheets of white construction paper, and have him or her draw a large dinosaur on one sheet of paper. Then have children completely cover the other sheet of paper with a heavy coating of chalk. Instruct them to cover the chalk with a heavy layer of crayon. Show how to lay the drawing, dinosaur side up, over the crayon and chalk paper, and trace over the drawing, pressing down hard. Remind children to trace over the details. When done, have children lift their drawings and turn over the paper. They will marvel at the two very different-looking prints!

Fossil Impressions

Materials:

- collection of washed and air-dried chicken, beef, and pork bones
- craft sticks
- water-based clay
- waxed paper

Give each child a sheet of waxed paper and a ball of clay.
Place a collection of bones in the middle of each group of children. Have them flatten their clay to make a smooth surface, and push different bones flat into the clay. Show how to carefully remove the bones to leave fossil-like impressions. Help children use craft sticks to carve their names in their plaques. Let the fossils dry. As a follow-up, set out the bones and plaques. Let children take turns matching the bones to their corresponding impressions.

Bulletin Boards

This wide variety of bulletin board displays provides cooperative interaction between you, and your students and the world of dinosaurs. These hands-on activities promote sharing among young children, as well as promoting the spirit of working together toward a common goal.

3-D Dinosaurs

Materials:

- butcher paper
- brown grocery bags
- paper and fabric scraps
- paper plates
- yarn
- black felt markers
- scissors
- glue
- stapler
- newspaper

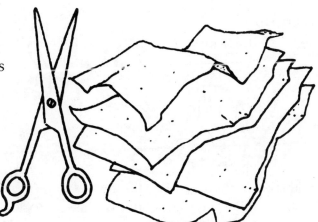

Cover a bulletin board with blue butcher paper. Use green and yellow paper to make leaves. Twist grocery bags and staple them to the board to form tree trunks. Add strips of green paper along the bottom for grass. Cut the paper plates in half and give each child two halves. Staple each pair of halves together along the edges, leaving an opening. Show children how to stuff newspaper in the opening to make a stuffed dinosaur body. Let children stuff their dinosaurs, and then staple the openings shut. Invite children to use yarn and paper and fabric scraps to add details, such as a head, legs, spikes, and a tail. Encourage children to use markers to add facial features and other details. Let children take turns talking about their dinosaurs.

Food for Dinosaurs

Materials:

- butcher paper
- black marker
- magazine pictures of different kinds of food
- pushpins

Cover a bulletin board with a light-colored butcher paper. Draw a line down the middle to form two columns. Print the word *MEAT* at the top of one column and *PLANTS* at the top of the other column. Pin pictures of vegetables, fruits, and meats around the border. Let children help you categorize the pictures in their appropriate columns. Once children become skilled at this activity, place the pictures in a box and let children take turns categorizing the pictures on the board.

Bulletin Boards

Dinosaur Hunt

Materials:

- different colored butcher paper
- cutout pictures of at least 20 dinosaurs
- markers
- tagboard squares
- pushpins
- hole punch
- scissors

Cover a bulletin board with butcher paper. Use different colors of butcher paper to make a lush-looking prehistoric habitat filled with ferns, trees, grasses, rocks, and lakes. Print the numbers *1–20* on separate tagboard squares, and punch a hole in the top of each square. Pin the dinosaurs within the habitat, partially hiding some of them behind bushes, rocks, and trees. (You might start by displaying only ten dinosaurs.) Then invite children to go on a dinosaur hunt! Encourage them to take turns finding dinosaurs in the habitat. Have the child who finds the first dinosaur hang Card 1 on its pin. Have the child who finds the second dinosaur place Card 2 on that dinosaur's pin, and so on. After the hunt is finished, have children count aloud in sequence as you point to each number card. This bulletin board game can be played again and again. Rearrange the dinosaurs for each round of play.

Dinosaur Sizes

Materials:

- butcher paper
- marker
- cutout pictures of big and little dinosaurs
- pushpins

Cover a bulletin board with butcher paper and add the title "Dinosaur Sizes." Using a marker, draw a line down the middle of the board. Print *Big* at the top of one side of the board and *Little* on the other side. Talk about how some dinosaurs were big and some were small. Hold up pictures of two different-sized dinosaurs, and let children tell you which is the larger animal. Let children take turns pinning each dinosaur in its appropriate column. As children become more skilled with this activity, randomly display the dinosaur cutouts and allow them to take turns arranging the cutouts in their correct columns.

As a follow-up activity, cut out pictures of medium-sized dinosaurs. This time divide your bulletin board into three columns, adding a middle column titled *Medium*. Hold up pictures of three different-sized dinosaurs and help children order the sizes from big to little. Pin each dinosaur in its appropriate column. Then let children take turns sorting and pinning up the rest of the dinosaurs.

Dinosaur Skin

Materials:
- butcher paper
- marker
- material scraps
  with different textures
- pushpins

Cover a bulletin board with butcher paper and add the title "Dinosaur Skin." Using a marker, draw a line down the middle of the board to make two columns. Print *Smooth* at the top of one column and *Rough* at the top of the other. Talk about how some dinosaurs probably had rough skin and some had smooth skin. Let children take turns naming things that are smooth and things that are rough. Hold up two different kinds of materials—one rough and one smooth. Let children tell you which is which. Then pin each material in the appropriate column. Place the rest of the materials in a box. Invite children to take turns touching different materials and categorizing them on the board.

Poetry Wall

Materials:
- butcher paper
- white
  unlined paper
- pencils
- crayons

Cover a bulletin board with butcher paper. Then prepare a poetry frame by printing the following:

Dino big,
Dino small,
Dino walk,
Dino call,
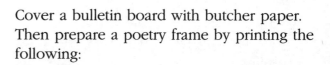

Marsha Elyn Wright

Reproduce the poetry frame for each child. Let children make up imaginative sounds that dinosaurs might have made. Practice making these dinosaur calls with the class. Then invite each child to make up a dinosaur "call" by writing it on the blank line in his or her frame. Have the child draw a picture of his or her dinosaur next to the poem. Let children share their poems and "calls" with the class. Post their poems on your bulletin board, adding the title "DINO Calls."

Bulletin Boards

Meat-Eaters and Plant-Eaters

Materials:
- butcher paper
- marker
- cutout dinosaur pictures
- pushpins

Cover a bulletin board with butcher paper. Draw a line down the middle of the board to make two columns. Print *Meat-Eaters* at the top of one column and *Plant-Eaters* at the top of the other. Tell children that some dinosaurs ate meat and had pointed, sharp teeth and claws to tear the meat. Each meat-eater had two large back legs that supported its body so it could move upright. Tell children that other dinosaurs were plant-eaters and had flat teeth for grinding plants. These dinosaurs walked on all four legs. Show a picture of a meat-eating dinosaur. Ask children: *Does this dinosaur have sharp teeth?* (yes) *Does it have two large back legs for walking upright?* (yes) *Is this dinosaur a meat-eater or a plant-eater?* (meat-eater) Repeat this activity with a picture of a plant-eating dinosaur. Invite different children to pin dinosaurs to their appropriate columns.

Days of the Dinosaurs

Materials:
- butcher paper
- mini sentence strips
- marker
- cutout dinosaur pictures
- pushpins

Create a prehistoric scene on a bulletin board and add the title "Days of the Dinosaurs." Each day, teach children about one kind of dinosaur and print its name on a sentence strip. Help children pronounce the dinosaur's name and learn about its interesting features and characteristics. Choose a child to pin the picture with its label in the prehistoric setting. This is a fun way for children to learn  about different kinds of dinosaurs and their names.

May I Keep It, Mom?

Materials:
- unlined paper
- construction paper
- crayons

Make a speech bubble pattern that reads: "May I keep it, Mom?" Add a writing line below the words. Reproduce this pattern for each child. Remind children that dinosaurs are no longer living. Then ask them: *Would dinosaurs have made good pets?* If possible, read aloud the book *Can I Have a Stegosaurus, Mom? Can I? Please!?* by Lois G. Grambling (Troll Associates, 1998). Let children draw themselves and their "pet" dinosaurs having fun together. Invite children to talk about their artwork.

Cooking

Experiences with food integrate all areas of the curriculum and meet the needs of the whole child. Food is a fun way to teach young children about the plant-eaters and meat-eaters of the prehistoric world!

Cooking

DINO-mite Shakes

Materials:

- 8-oz. plastic cups
- teaspoons
- milk
- vanilla ice cream (about one gallon of milk and one half-gallon of ice cream for 20 children)
- markers
- ice-cream scoop
- chopped fresh fruit
- sprinkles
- paper towels

Have children wash their hands. Mark a line on each cup about three inches from the bottom. Set up an assembly line. Place cups, ice cream, milk, chopped fruit, sprinkles, and spoons in a line in the middle of a table. Let children walk on both sides of the table to create their milkshakes. Demonstrate how to put one scoop of ice cream in a cup, pour milk up to the marked line, and add fruit and/or sprinkles. Tell children to stir their ice-cream mixtures until they become smooth. Enjoy!

Dinosaur Grins

Materials:

- apple slices (two per child)
- mini marshmallows
- peanut butter
- plastic knives
- paper towels

Have children wash their hands. Then give each child two apple slices. Have him or her spread peanut butter on one side of each slice. Help children add marshmallow "teeth" to one slice, and then press the slices together to form a dinosaur grin!

Graham Cracker and Peanut Butter Dinosaurs

Materials:

- paper plates
- graham crackers
- peanut butter
- raisins
- plastic knives and spoons
- paper towels

Give each child a paper towel, a knife and spoon, a paper plate, a big dollop of peanut butter, two graham crackers, and some raisins. Let children make shapes out of their graham crackers by breaking them apart, arranging the shapes, and "gluing" them together with peanut butter to make their own dinosaurs. Encourage children to use raisins for eyes, noses, toes, claws, and spikes.

Meat or Vegetable?

Materials:

- washed, cut-up vegetables
- cooked, cut-up turkey, ham, and beef
- tray
- paper bowls
- plastic forks
- napkins

Make sure children wash their hands. Place some vegetables and pieces of meat on a tray. Have children name the food and decide if it is a meat or vegetable. With children, count the vegetables and the meat. Make tally marks for each. Repeat this activity with a different selection of meats and vegetables. Afterwards, let children select various meats and vegetables to place in bowls and eat during snack time.

Growing Herbs

Materials:

- clean egg cartons (one per child)
- potting soil
- tablespoons
- herb seeds
- two or three spray bottles with water
- newspaper

Talk with children about how people use plants, or herbs, to season food. Remind children that some dinosaurs ate only plants. Tell children that they are going to plant their own herb gardens. Demonstrate how to put a spoonful of soil into each section of an egg carton, sprinkle herb seeds in the soil, and place another spoonful of soil on top of the seeds. After children plant their seeds, let them take turns spraying water on the soil. Place the cartons near a sunny window and check them daily. Let children spray water on their gardens when necessary. When the herbs are full-grown, let children cut them up and store them in plastic bags. Invite them to smell, taste, and touch the herbs before taking them home.

Cooking

Prehistoric Soil

Materials:

- paper cups
- plastic spoons
- paper towels
- milk
- chocolate instant pudding
- large bowl
- wire whisk
- whipped topping
- chocolate cookies broken into pieces
- "gummy" worms and bugs
- granola
- nuts
- small bowls

Combine chocolate pudding and milk according to package directions. Use a wire whisk to mix. Let the mixture sit for five minutes. Place cookie pieces, candy, granola, and nuts in separate bowls. Let each child place chocolate pudding in a cup and add whipped topping. Then have him or her spoon candy, cookie pieces, and nuts into their cups to make "prehistoric soil." Invite children to eat and enjoy their special treats!

Trail Mix

Materials:

- paper cups
- plastic spoons
- paper towels
- small bowls
- nuts
- dried fruit
- seeds
- granola
- chocolate pieces

Tell children they are going on a dinosaur hunt and will snack on trail mix along the way. Place the different ingredients in separate bowls. Set up an assembly line, so children can select their food items from both sides of a serving table. Give each child a cup with his or her name printed on it. Then have children select and put different food items in their cups. (HINT: Before the hike, hide some stuffed dinosaurs in the playground.) Take children on a "hike" around the playground and encourage them to search for dinosaurs while snacking.

Memory Fun

Materials:

- serving tray
- various kinds of bread
- cake and cookie dough
- dinosaur cookie cutters

Use dinosaur cookie cutters to make dinosaur shapes from different kinds of bread, cake, and cookie dough. (Note: If you use cookie dough, make sure to bake the cookies.) Place the items on the tray. Encourage children to describe their colors, shapes, textures, and smells. Then have them close their eyes while you remove one of the items. When children open their eyes, they must study the tray to discover which item is missing. Repeat this over and over. As children get more skilled at this game, add more food items.

Food Collages

Materials:

- magazine pictures of a variety of foods
- newspaper food ads
- glue
- scissors
- construction paper

Remind children that some dinosaurs ate meat and some ate plants. Talk about foods that are meats and foods that are plants. Show children examples of each category using magazine pictures. Give children magazines, newspapers, glue, scissors, and construction paper. Encourage them to cut out lots of food pictures to glue on the paper to make a collage. Demonstrate how to cut out the pictures in a variety of fun shapes and overlap them on the paper. Depending on children's abilities, you might have them cut out food words to glue on their collages as well.

Dinosaur Placemats

Materials:

- paint smocks
- construction paper
- thick tempera paint
- squeeze bottles with small openings (empty mustard, ketchup, and detergent bottles work well)
- black markers
- clear contact paper
- newspapers

Have children wear paint smocks, and cover the work area with newspaper. Pour each color of paint into a separate bottle. Demonstrate how to fold a paper in half "like a hamburger bun," and then unfold it. Let children squirt dabs of different colored paint onto one half of his or her paper, and fold the paper again. Tell children to press the paper together to smear the paint. Then have them carefully open the paper and see the exciting results! Encourage children to use markers to create an imaginative dinosaur out of the smeared picture. Help children print their names on their placemats. Let dry. Cover each mat with clear contact paper for durability.

Marshmallow Creatures

Materials:

- large and mini marshmallows
- toothpicks
- paper plates

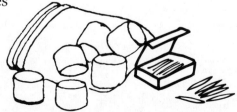

Display pictures of various dinosaurs and talk with children about their different sizes and shapes. Demonstrate how to join marshmallows with toothpicks to create legs, a neck, and a tail for an imaginative dinosaur. Then allow children to use the materials to create their own creatures. Display each dinosaur on a paper plate. Invite children to enjoy their sweet treats!

Dramatic Play

One of the most effective ways young children learn is through dramatic play. These role-playing experiences help develop the whole child physically, emotionally, socially, and cognitively. And—children will have a great time!

DINO Dig

Wash and air-dry several chicken, beef, and pork bones. Bury them in the sand in the playground. Show children pictures of dinosaur fossils. Tell them that these fossils help us learn about the dinosaurs that lived long ago. Have children pretend they are paleontologists going on a dinosaur dig. Give each child a spoon to dig in the sand. Then take children out into the playground and have them scoop up sand to uncover the bones. After they've made most of the discoveries, invite them to take turns talking about the size and shape of the different bones. Remind children that dinosaur bones were much, much bigger!

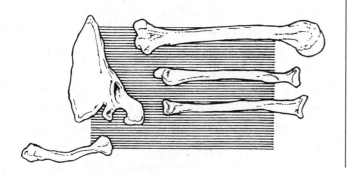

Hungry Dinosaurs

Cut out pictures of meats, fruits, and vegetables. Glue each picture to construction paper for durability. Then hide the pictures around the room. Place children in two groups—plant-eaters and meat-eaters—and have them sit in a circle. Let children pretend to be hungry dinosaurs searching for food. Have the plant-eaters move on "all fours" and the meat-eaters move upright. Encourage each child to find one picture of the type of food he or she might eat. After finding the appropriate food, have the child return to the circle of dinosaurs. Let children take turns describing the kind of foods they found.

Stomping Dinosaurs!

Collect shoeboxes with lids, so each child has a pair. Use masking tape to secure the lids to the boxes. Cut a hole in the top of the boxes so a child can slip his or her feet through the holes. Play lively music and encourage children to step into their boxes and stomp around the room, pretending to be dinosaurs roaming the earth. Stomp! Stomp!

Dramatic Play

Dinosaur Days

Display pictures of dinosaurs. Let children look carefully at the dinosaurs' characteristics and describe them—long necks, short necks, long tails, short tails, sharp teeth, flat teeth, horns, and so on. If appropriate, teach children the name of each dinosaur. Tell them that scientists don't know what kinds of sounds dinosaurs made. Invite children to "become" the dinosaurs they explored. Have children who are plant-eaters move slowly on their hands and knees. Have the "meat-eaters" move upright. Encourage children to make up sounds and calls that the dinosaurs might have made, and then move around the room, hooting and snorting like dinosaurs!

Fruit and Vegetable Stand

Remind children that some dinosaurs only ate fruits, vegetables, grasses, leaves, and other plants. Set up a vegetable market using a table and plastic or real fruits and vegetables. Let children take turns being the owner who sells the produce. Invite other children to pretend they are plant-eating dinosaurs shopping for food. Encourage children to describe the produce they purchased. If real food is used, let children enjoy a healthy snack after everyone has had a turn shopping!

Building a Museum

Collect several toy dinosaurs. Have children pretend that they are building a dinosaur museum. Using toy construction gear and equipment, let children arrange wooden blocks into a "museum" structure. Have them display the dinosaurs in their museum. You might even label each dinosaur and provide some simple facts. Let children take turns playing tour guide. Invite another class to tour your dinosaur museum, too!

Romp of the Dinosaurs

Go out on the playground and let children practice moving like different kinds of dinosaurs. Have them form a line and sing "Stomp, Stomp, Stomp Your Feet." Invite children to act out the words as you sing together.

Stomp, Stomp, Stomp Your Feet
(Sung to the tune "Row, Row, Row Your Boat")

Stomp, stomp, stomp your feet,
Quickly on your toes,
Merrily, merrily, merrily, merrily,
Dinosaurs unfroze!

Clomp, clomp, clomp your feet,
Slowly on all fours,
Merrily, merrily, merrily, merrily,
Dinosaurs galore!

Marsha Elyn Wright

Who Am I?

Remind children that meat-eating dinosaurs walked upright, moved quickly, and had sharp teeth and claws; and that plant-eating dinosaurs moved on all fours, walked slowly, and had flat teeth for grinding plants. Have children sit in a circle. Ask a couple of volunteers to move to the center of the circle and pretend to be either meat-eating or plant-eating dinosaurs. Play some lively music and encourage the "dinosaurs" to play their parts by moving around. When the music stops, have the other children try to guess what kind of dinosaur each child pretended to be. Repeat the activity, allowing different children to move like dinosaurs.

Dramatic Play

DINO Puppets

Display pictures of dinosaurs. Talk with children about different dinosaur characteristics—long and short necks, long tails, big or little legs, and so on. Cut out a generic dinosaur pattern, making each child a dinosaur. Have each child glue a craft stick to the back of his or her dinosaur to make a puppet. Invite children to use paper scraps and crayons to add tails, plates, spikes, and other details to their dinosaurs. Hang a blanket over a table for a puppet stage, and have small groups of children take turns performing dinosaur puppet plays!

Fast and Slow

Remind children that plant-eating dinosaurs probably moved very slowly on all four legs, and meat-eating dinosaurs most likely moved quickly on two strong back legs. Have children pretend to be dinosaurs. When you call out, "Slow," have children get on their hands and knees and move slowly. Each time you call out, "Slow," have children move slower and slower. Then call out, "Fast," and have children move quickly in an upright position. Each time you call out, "Fast," have children move faster and faster. After practicing this game a few times, randomly call out "Slow" and "Fast," and have children move accordingly.

Dinosaur Pantomime

Encourage children to help you think of all the things a dinosaur could do—stand on its hind legs and eat leaves from trees, roll on its back, and so on. Invite a volunteer to stand in the middle of a circle and act out the movements to some activity a dinosaur might have done. See how long it takes the other children to guess what the dinosaur is doing!

DINO Fingerplays

Perform the following fingerplays
with children.

Hungry Dinosaur

One claw,
> *(Hold out one hand like a claw.)*

Two claws,
> *(Hold out other hand like a claw.)*

Stretching out to grab,
> *(Reach out hands, moving fingers.)*

Tiptoe, tiptoe,
> *(Move in place on tiptoes.)*

Hungry for a meal!
> *(Growl!)*

Marsha Elyn Wright

Two Dinosaurs

One little dinosaur,
> *(Hold up one finger on left hand, like a puppet.)*

Looking for a friend,
> *(Move finger back and forth as if looking for something.)*

Sees another dinosaur,
> *(Hold up one finger on right hand like a puppet.)*

Big from end to end,
> *(Slowly move finger on right hand.)*

Dinosaurs play,
> *(Move both fingers.)*

Dinosaurs eat,
> *(Make eating noises.)*

Now they're friends,
> *(Move both fingers, side by side.)*

Isn't that sweet!
> *(Say, "Ahhh!")*

Marsha Elyn Wright

Dramatic Play

Dinosaur Maze

Show children a picture of an Ankylosaurus (ang-KILE-uh-sor-us). Encourage children to describe this dinosaur—rows of short spikes covering its body, bony club at the end of its tail, walked on all fours, sharp claws. Tell children that many dinosaurs hatched from eggs, and this dinosaur was one of them. Set up a maze of cardboard boxes. Place inflated balloons on a nest of "paper" grass at the end of the maze. Have children take turns pretending to be an Ankylosaurus searching for its nest of eggs. Let children, one by one, enter the maze and make his or her way through it to the nest. Add excitement and fun by timing each child's journey!

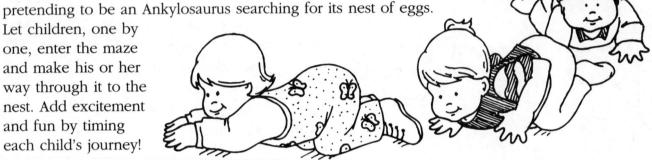

Dinosaur Defenses

Tell children that plant-eating dinosaurs had different and unique ways of protecting themselves—sharp horns to scare away enemies; long, spiked tails to poke, whip, and fight off meat-eating predators; and club tails to swing at enemies. Have children pretend to be plant-eating dinosaurs. When you call out, "Meat-eaters," have children use their bodies to protect themselves like dinosaurs might have done long ago.

Dino Zoo

Invite children to create a dinosaur zoo! Display and talk about different kinds of dinosaurs. Have some children acts as dinosaurs, other children act as visitors to the zoo, and a few act as zookeepers. Let them use wooden blocks and/or cardboard boxes to set up dinosaur displays and "fences." Give children lots of time to play in their pretend zoo. If time permits, invite them to switch roles.

If You're Scared

Display pictures of dinosaurs. Tell children that because there aren't any dinosaurs living today to observe, scientists aren't sure how they behaved or even looked. Scientists try to guess how dinosaurs acted by studying present-day animal behavior. Before singing "If You're Scared and You Know It," have children pretend to be dinosaurs, moving about on all fours as plant-eaters or upright as meat-eaters. As you sing, have children act out the words.

If You're Scared and You Know It
(Sung to the tune "If You're Happy and You Know It")

If you're scared and you know it, move your claws,
If you're scared and you know it, move your claws,
If you're scared and you know it,
Then your claws will surely show it,
If you're scared and you know it, move your claws!

If you're scared and you know it, point your horns,
If you're scared and you know it, point your horns,
If you're scared and you know it,
Then your horns will surely show it,
If you're scared and you know it, point your horns!

If you're scared and you know it, swing your tail,
If you're scared and you know it, swing your tail,
If you're scared and you know it,
Then your tail will surely show it,
If you're scared and you know it, swing your tail!

If you're scared and you know it, roar out loud,
If you're scared and you know it, roar out loud,
If you're scared and you know it,
Then your voice will surely show it,
If you're scared and you know it, roar out loud!

Marsha Elyn Wright

Dramatic Play

Egg to Dinosaur

Use a jump rope to make a large circle on the floor. Designate this circle as a dinosaur nest. Tell children to pretend they are dinosaur eggs ready to hatch inside the nest. Have children "scrunch down," with arms close to their sides, as if they are inside eggs. Have them slowly begin to rock back and forth, rolling very carefully. Encourage children to slowly "crack" their eggshells and emerge as baby dinosaurs. Let children share what kinds of dinosaurs they are.

Run, Dinosaurs, Run!

Tell children that in the days of the dinosaurs, meat-eaters chased and tried to eat plant-eating dinosaurs. Lay two long clotheslines on the grass about 20 feet apart. Choose two or three children to act as meat-eating dinosaur, and have them stand in between the two clotheslines. Tell the other children to stand outside the clotheslines, some on one side and some on the other. They will be plant-eating dinosaurs. When you call out, "Run, dinosaurs, run," have the "plant-eaters" try to run to the other clothesline without getting tagged by the "meat-eaters." When a meat-eater tags a plant-eater, the plant-eater must freeze. At the start of the next round of play, the tagged plant-eaters become meat-eaters who try to tag as many of the remaining plant-eaters as they can. Keep playing more and more rounds until all the plant-eaters are caught!

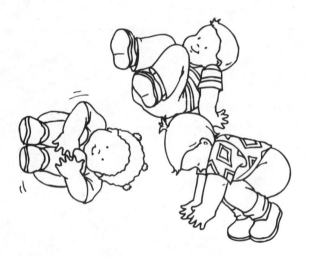

Watch Out!

Remind children that many plant-eating dinosaurs probably used their tails to protect themselves against meat-eating dinosaurs. Then play this fun outdoor game. Tie a shoe to the end of a long jump rope to form the "tail" of a plant-eating dinosaur. Have children pretend to be meat-eating dinosaurs and stand in a circle around you. Hold the shoeless end of the rope and spin around slowly so the shoe moves in a circle, close to the ground. Have children jump over the "tail" as it passes under them.

Dinosaurs on the Move

Explain to children that different dinosaurs moved in a variety of ways. Ask children to move like dinosaurs as you read the following descriptions:

Plateosaurus (PLAY-tee-oh-SOR-us)—was a plant-eater that slowly walked on all fours. When it wanted to eat leaves on tall trees, it would stand up on its hind legs and stretch up to reach them.

Coelophysis (SEEL-oh-FIE-sis)—was a meat-eater that walked upright on the toes of its hind feet. It leaned forward, using its tail for balance. It could run very fast!

Herrerasaurus (heh-reh-rah-SOR-us)—was a meat-eater that walked upright on the toes of its hind legs. It leaned forward, using its tail for balance. It had short arms and claws. Because its arms were so short, they weren't very useful. It could also move very quickly!

Plant-Eaters Relay Race

Tell children that plant-eating dinosaurs walked on all four legs and usually had flat feet. Let children pretend to be plant-eating dinosaurs with flat feet. Make two pairs of "flat feet" per child by cutting two sturdy paper plates into halves. For each foot, place one half of a paper plate facedown on top of a whole paper plate, lining up the edges. Punch holes through both rims and lace yarn tightly through the holes. Your "feet" will look like paper slippers! Place children in two teams, and have them line up next to each other. Lay a jump rope down at the starting line and place orange cones about ten feet away from the starting line. At your signal, have the first dinosaur in each group slip on the paper-plate feet, walk to the cones, return to his or her line, and give the "feet" to the next child in line. Continue until every child has had a turn.

Dramatic Play

Just Like Mama

Tell children that young dinosaurs probably learned how to move, hunt, eat, and protect themselves by watching and imitating their parents. Discuss with children the kinds of things they learn how to do from watching their parents—eat, wash, brush teeth, get dressed, and so on. Have children pretend to be baby dinosaurs. Let them form a circle around you, the "mama." Perform a movement or make a sound like a dinosaur, and have children imitate you. Once children become more skilled at this activity, let volunteers take turns being the mama dinosaur.

Dinosaur, Dinosaur, Turn Around

As you recite this rhyme, based on the familiar chant "Teddy Bear," invite children to act out the words. Depending on the children's abilities, you might try teaching them the rhyme so they can chant along with you.

Dinosaur, dinosaur, turn around,
Dinosaur, dinosaur, touch the ground,
Dinosaur, dinosaur, show your feet,
Dinosaur, dinosaur, eat and eat!

Dinosaur, dinosaur, roar out loud,
Dinosaur, dinosaur, stand real proud,
Dinosaur, dinosaur, stretch out long,
Dinosaur, dinosaur, you are strong!

Dinosaur, dinosaur, swing your tail,
Dinosaur, dinosaur, wail and wail,
Dinosaur, dinosaur, claw and dig,
Dinosaur, dinosaur, stand up big!

Marsha Elyn Wright

Big and Little Dinosaurs

Have children pretend to be dinosaurs as they act out the words to this familiar tune.

Big and Little Dinosaurs

(Sung to the tune "Twinkle, Twinkle, Little Star")

Big and scary dinosaurs,
Show your claws and give a roar,
Run so fast on two back feet,
Eating meat is such a treat,
Big and scary dinosaurs,
Show your claws and give a roar!

Long and spiky dinosaurs,
Show your horns and give a roar,
Move so slowly on four feet,
Eating plants is such a treat,
Long and spiky dinosaurs,
Show your horns and give a roar!

Marsha Elyn Wright

Dinosaur Charades

Brainstorm with children and make a list of dinosaur actions, such as the following:

- Swing its tail
- Dig with its claws
- Move slowly on all fours
- Tear at meat
- "Honk" with its horn
- Hatch from an egg
- Stretch its neck
- Run on its hind legs
- Chew plants
- Stand on tiptoes to reach tall plants
- Build a mud nest
- Roar loudly

Then invite children to take turns performing one of the actions. Let the rest of the class guess the activity. Whoever is first to guess correctly gets to perform next!

Dramatic Play

Let's Hide!

Use a large, round tablecloth or parachute for this outdoor game. Have children pretend to be plant-eating dinosaurs that hide from enemies underneath a huge bush! Let each child stand around the tablecloth, grab hold of it with both hands, and lift it waist high. Tell children that when you call out, "Hide, dinosaurs, hide," they should lift the tablecloth over their heads, and then sit down and let the tablecloth fall over them. Children will want to play this again and again. You might choose different children to call out "Hide" each time you play.

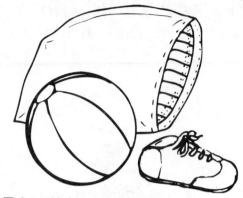

"Tar Pits" Obstacle Course

Tell children that some dinosaurs got stuck, and often died in soft, quick-sinking pits made of black tar. Set up an obstacle course on the grass or playground. Randomly place gym shoes, pillows, and other soft items along the course. Have children pretend to be dinosaurs that walk along the path, trying to stay out of the tar pits (obstacles). Have children walk the path, blindfolded, one at a time. Appoint some children to sit along the path and call out directions so the walker doesn't step on an obstacle. Repeat this game so everyone has a turn walking the obstacle course.

Dinosaur Pals

Have children pair off as "dinosaur pals." Tell partners to explore different ways young dinosaurs might have played together—moving with elbows hooked, walking back to back, gently pushing head to head, and so on. Give children some time to experiment, and then invite volunteers to take turns showing the rest of the class their creative playtime fun.

Language Arts

These meaningful language activities emphasize the close relationship between speaking, listening, writing, and reading. The ideas offer young children opportunities to speak and write about the world around them as they develop language skills.

Language Arts

Spelling DINOSAUR

This is a fun way to help children recognize the word *dinosaur*. First, cut tissue paper into two-inch squares. On a strip of tagboard, make wide letters that spell *dinosaur*. Copy the pattern onto wide strips of light-colored construction paper, so each child has a strip. Have children take the tissue paper squares and roll them with their fingers into round balls. Demonstrate how to squeeze glue down the middle of each letter in *dinosaur* and press the tissue paper balls onto the glue. Let dry. Invite children to hold up their artwork and spell the word *dinosaur*, pointing to each letter as they say it.

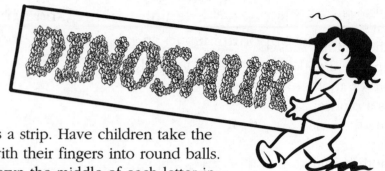

DINO Puzzles

Here's a simple way for each child to make his or her own dinosaur puzzle. Make a simple puzzle grid with wide cutting lines. Copy it for each child. Then have each child draw and color a dinosaur on the blank side of the puzzle paper. Ask children to turn over their puzzle papers and cut on the lines. Give each child an envelope in which to store his or her puzzle. Help children print their names on their envelopes. Then let children spend time trading and solving each other's puzzles!

Memory Match

Make a set of 20 tagboard squares. Buy enough dinosaur stickers so you have two stickers each of ten different dinosaurs. Place a sticker on each tagboard square to make ten matching pairs of dinosaur cards. Demonstrate how to play the following game: Show children how to shuffle the cards and place them facedown in rows. Then choose a child to turn over two cards. Tell children that if the dinosaurs match, the player who picked the cards gets to keep them and takes another turn. Explain that if the dinosaurs don't match, the player returns the cards, facedown, and it's the next player's turn. Tell children to keep taking turns until all the cards are matched. Place the cards in a box at a center, so children can play the game during free activity time.

Is It a Dinosaur?

This is a good visual discrimination activity that's simple to prepare. Buy dinosaur and other animal stickers. Place the stickers on separate tagboard squares. Hold up a picture of another animal, and ask children if it's a dinosaur. Let children give reasons why the animal is not a dinosaur. Then display three dinosaur cards and one card of another animal. Ask children to tell you which card shows an animal that isn't a dinosaur. As children get better at identifying dinosaurs, play the game by mixing in more than one animal card with the dinosaur cards. You might let children take turns choosing which cards to display for the rest of the class.

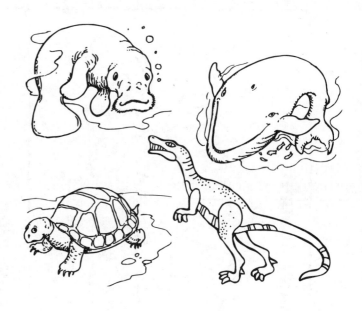

Dinosaur Dictionary

Let children make their own books about dinosaurs! Reproduce "My Dinosaur Dictionary" on pages 42 and 43 for each child. Let children color the pictures, cut them out, and staple them into small books. Read the books together several times before having children take them home to share with their families!

Dinosaur Puppets

Have children make simple dinosaur puppets. Reproduce "My Dinosaur Dictionary" on pages 42 and 43 for each child. Let children color the pictures and cut them out. Demonstrate how to glue a craft stick to the back of each dinosaur. Let dry. Encourage children to make up stories with their dinosaur puppets. Then invite them to perform their stories for the class or their parents.

Language Arts

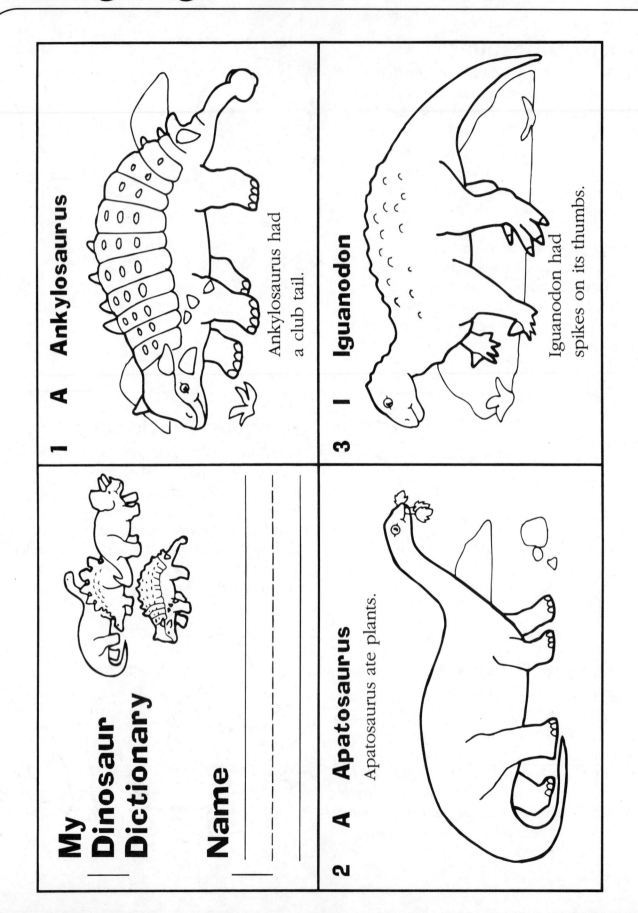

My Dinosaur Dictionary

Name _____

1 A Ankylosaurus

Ankylosaurus had a club tail.

2 A Apatosaurus

Apatosaurus ate plants.

3 I Iguanodon

Iguanodon had spikes on its thumbs.

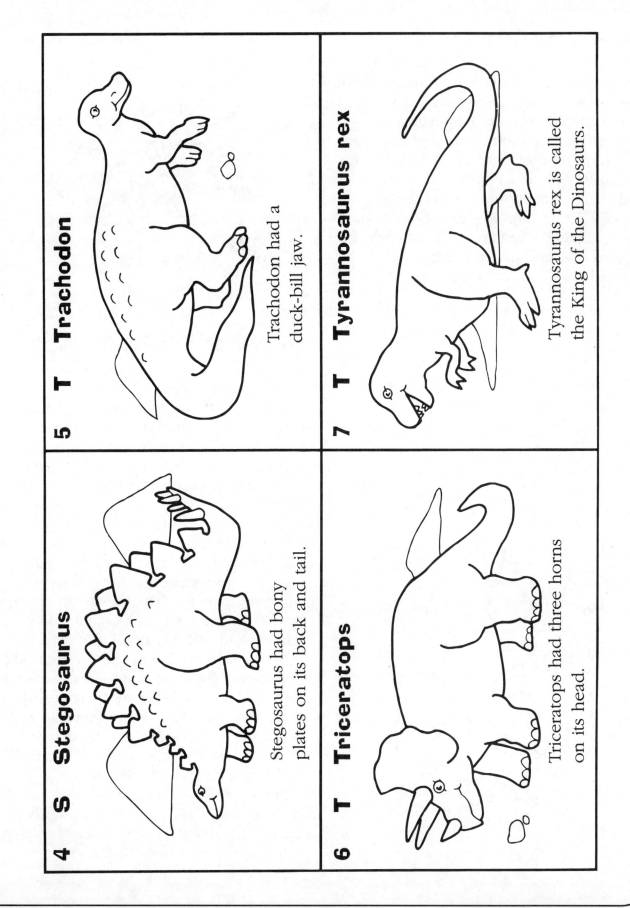

4 S Stegosaurus

Stegosaurus had bony plates on its back and tail.

5 T Trachodon

Trachodon had a duck-bill jaw.

6 T Triceratops

Triceratops had three horns on its head.

7 T Tyrannosaurus rex

Tyrannosaurus rex is called the King of the Dinosaurs.

Language Arts

Magnetic Play

Use metallic surfaces, such as cookie sheets or pizza pans, and several sets of magnetic alphabet letters for children to practice spelling simple dinosaur-related words. Print multiples of easy words (big, tall, short, small, teeth, tail, eyes, horn) on strips of tagboard, and glue a strip of magnetic tape on the back of each strip. Draw a simple illustration of each word on the card. Place a set of strips on each magnetic board. Have children take turns finding the matching magnetic letters and placing them below the printed letters on each card.

| A | is for _____ . |

| A | is for _____ . |

| A | is for _____ . |

A

| A | is for _____ . |

| A | is for _____ . |

| A | is for _____ . |

Alphabet Dinosaur Wall

Make an ABC mural about dinosaurs! Photocopy the sentence frames on page 48, and print a different letter of the alphabet in each box. Make enough copies for every letter of the alphabet. Then make enough copies, so each child has a set of 26 sentence frames. Let children cut out the frames and store them in envelopes. Print children's names on their envelopes. Spotlight each letter one at a time. Begin by displaying a sheet of bright-colored butcher paper on a wall. Draw a large outline of a dinosaur on the paper and print the featured letter on its body. Then brainstorm a list of dinosaur-related words that begin with that letter (see "ABC Books" activity, page 46, for examples). Help each child complete his or her sentence frame with one of the words from the list. Next, have children take turns pinning his or her sentence on the dinosaur. Encourage children to illustrate their sentences on the butcher paper. Remind children to "sign" their names by their artwork! Review the mural each day. When children are ready to study the next letter, put up different-colored butcher paper and repeat the process!

Dinosaur Books to Share

While studying the exciting world of dinosaurs, gather children on the rug and read aloud factual, fun, and fascinating books about these amazing prehistoric creatures. Here are a few titles to help you get started on your read-aloud collection.

Can I Have a Stegosaurus, Mom? Can I? Please!? by Lois G. Grambling
(Troll Associates, 1998)

Digging Up Dinosaurs by Aliki
(HarperTrophy, 1988)

The Dinosaur Who Lived in My Backyard by B. G. Hennessy
(Puffin, 1990)

Dinosaurs Roar! by Paul and Henrietta Stickland
(Dutton Books, 1997)

Fossils Tell of Long Ago by Aliki
(HarperTrophy, 1990)

Patrick's Dinosaurs by Carol Carrick
(Houghton Mifflin Co., 1985)

The Smallest Stegosaurus by Lynn Sweat and Louis Phillips
(Puffin, 1995)

Recording Books

This activity helps develop children's listening skills and teaches children the beginning steps to reading. Tape-record your favorite dinosaur books, making a distinctive sound (bell ringing, cat meowing) when a child should turn the page. Then place each story tape with its corresponding book in a basket at your reading center. Demonstrate how to follow the words in the book while listening to the accompanying tape and how to turn the pages when the sound is made.

Language Arts

ABC Books

Make a blank 26-page book for each child. Help children print *ABC Book* and their names on their book covers. Then have children work on one page of their books at a time, studying each letter of the alphabet in relationship to dinosaurs (*A is for Apatosaurus, B is for BIG, C is for claws, D is for dinosaur*). Photocopy the sentence frames (page 48), and print in the box the alphabet letter you are studying. Next, make enough copies so each child has one sentence frame. Demonstrate how to glue the sentence frame (*A is for _____*) on the first page of their books. Then brainstorm with children several dinosaur-related words that begin with *a—awesome, Allosaurus, Apatosaurus*. Help each child complete his or her sentence frame with one of the words, and then illustrate the sentence. Encourage children to "read" their book pages to each other as they finish them. When all the pages are complete, invite parents for "Author's Day." Ask children to share their books with their families. This is a great way to communicate to parents what children have been learning.

Story Time Extended

When you finish reading a book about dinosaurs, make time to let children use simple props to reenact what happened in the story. Also, go back and summarize what happened in the beginning, middle, and end of the story. If you read a book more than once, you might let children take turns acting out what is happening in the story while you are reading it again. Remind them of the movements and sounds dinosaurs might have made. If time permits, pause occasionally during your reading of the book and ask children about what is happening or what will happen next. This helps to keep children focused on the story and develops their ability to reason and predict.

Dinosaur ABCs

Invite children to make *"Dinosaur ABCs"* books. Spotlight one letter at a time. Post the following text, one line at a time, on chart paper. Photocopy the sentence frames (page 48), and print the letter you are studying inside each box. Make a copy for each child. Then help children complete the sentence frames, and glue them at the top of the corresponding page in their books. Tell children to illustrate their sentences, and then take home their books to share with their families.

Dinosaur ABCs

A is for awesome,
B is for bones,
C is for claws,
D is for dinosaur.

E is for eggs,
F is for fossil,
G is for GIANT,
H is for horns.

I is for intelligent,
J is for jump,
K is for kick,
L is for long.

M is for meat,
N is for noisy,
O is for old,
P is for plants.

Q is for quick,
R is for run,
S is for spikes,
T is for tail.

U is for unusual,
V is for VERY BIG,
W is for walk,
X is for X-ray.

Y is for young,
Z is for zoom!

Marsha Elyn Wright

Language Arts

Sentence Frames

 is for _____.

☐ is for _____.

☐ is for _____.

 is for _____.

Teacher: Use these sentence frames for activities on pages 44, 46, and 47.

1-57029-483-6 *Theme-a-Saurus: Dinosaurs*

Sticker Books

Demonstrate how to make a blank book by putting half-sized sheets of paper together, adding a construction paper cover, and stapling the pages together along the left-hand side. Plan enough time for each child to make a book. Then give children a variety of dinosaur stickers. Let children decorate the pages of their books by pressing on stickers and drawing dinosaur pictures. Help them print their names and books titles on the front covers. When children are finished with their books, host an "Author's Day." Encourage children to "read" their dinosaur stories to the rest of the class.

Did you find the D?

Letter Hunt

Print the letters of the word *dinosaur* and other letters on separate self-stick notes. Stick the notes around the room where children can easily see them. Choose one child to be the Hunter. If possible, give the Hunter a net (toy net for catching butterflies) and a magnifying glass. Tell the Hunter to walk around the room and look for the letter *d*. When the Hunter finds the *d*, he or she "captures" it and brings it to you. Choose the next Hunter, who will then search for the letter *i*. Continue playing the game until each letter in the word *dinosaur* is found.

Fingerprinting DINOSAUR

Print the word *dinosaur* in large letters on strips of paper, one strip per child. Set out inkpads and paper towels. Demonstrate how to press a finger on the inkpad, and then "trace" over each letter in the word *dinosaur* by stamping on fingerprints.

DINOSAUR

Language Arts

There Once Was a Dinosaur

Have fun on a rainy day by telling a round-robin dinosaur tale. Have children sit in a circle. Place a drum in front of you. Begin a steady beat and chant the following rhyme:

There once was a dinosaur,
That greeted me with a roar!
I shouted and ran,
Tripping over a can,
And this is what it did . . .

Marsha Elyn Wright

Let children take turns telling what the dinosaur did. After each child makes up his or her part of the story, chant the rhyme again for the next child. This round-robin storytelling is such fun that children will want to do it on sunny days, too!

Story Mats

Make story mats by creating simple outdoor scenes on 12-inch by 18-inch sheets of blue construction paper. Make different scenes by cutting out and gluing on different paper shapes, such as snowflakes, grassy hills, tall trees, and lakes. Create a different scene on each side of the mat. Next, cover each story mat with self-stick, clear contact paper for durability. Then cut out paper or "fun foam" shapes of dinosaurs, clouds, bushes, trees, and so on. Place sets of shapes in separate boxes. Let children take turns choosing a story mat and a box of shapes. Invite children to make up stories as they manipulate the shapes on their story mats. Provide time for children to share their stories with the class.

Before and After

Gather children together in a circle on the rug. Show them a scene featuring dinosaurs. Ask children: *What are the dinosaurs doing? What do you think happened before? What do you think will happen after?* This activity helps children develop their creative thinking as well as predicting skills.

These hands-on, interactive activities help young children develop pre-math and basic math skills while they explore the fascinating world of dinosaurs.

Math

Counting Dinosaurs

Buy a bag of peanuts in their shells. Use unlined index cards to make a set of counting cards. Draw one circle on one index card, two circles on a second card, three circles on a third card, and so on, up to ten cards. Lay the cards on a table in sequential order. Place the peanuts in a basket. Tell children to pretend the peanuts are dinosaurs. Have them take turns counting the peanuts as they place them in the circles on the cards.

How Many Plates?

Cut out a large, simple shape of a dinosaur with a long tail (such as a Stegosaurus). Cut out 10 to 20 paper triangles to use as dinosaur plates. Display the dinosaur on a wall. Ask a child to pin a specified number of "plates" along the dinosaur's back and tail. With the class, count the plates as you remove them from the dinosaur. Repeat this activity by asking children to place different numbers of plates on the dinosaur. Continue until each child has had a turn.

Dinosaur Patterns

Buy multiple copies of dinosaur stickers. Cut tagboard into small squares and attach one sticker to each square. Make simple patterns for children to duplicate by taping the squares, side by side, on separate lengths of yarn. Let children take turns lining up their own set of dinosaur squares to duplicate each pattern.

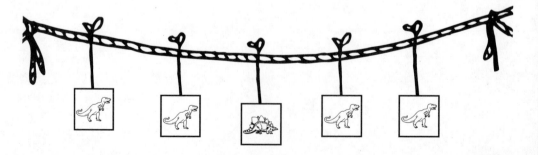

Dinosaur Match-ups

Enlarge and photocopy the dinosaur cards (pages 54 and 55) on sturdy paper. Color each dinosaur a different color. Cut out the cards, and then cut each card in half. Mix up the halves and lay them on a table. Let children take turns putting the dinosaur cards back together by matching the colors and body shapes on the cards.

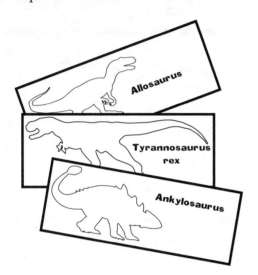

Dinosaur Counting . . . and More!

Enlarge and photocopy the dinosaur cards from pages 54 and 55 so there are 10 to 20 in all. Color and cut out the cards, and laminate them. Place 10 to 20 dinosaur cards in a line on the floor. Let children take turns going from one square to the next, counting aloud as they go. Use this same activity to teach children how to add on one or more. Choose a child to start with the first square. Say to the child: *Move up three squares. Count as you go.* Have the rest of the class count with the child. Then say: *You counted to three. Move up one more square and add on one more to your number.* Have the child move up one square and say his or her new number (*four*). Repeat this activity several times to help children understand how to add on one or more.

Dinosaur Concentration

Photocopy two sets of the dinosaur cards from pages 54 and 55 onto sturdy paper. Color and cut out the cards. Mix up the cards and lay them facedown on a table or the floor. Choose one child to turn over two cards. If the dinosaurs match, the child keeps the cards. Then choose the next child to turn over two cards. If the dinosaurs don't match, the child returns both cards, facedown, exactly where they were. Continue playing until all the cards have been matched. If every child didn't get a chance to choose two cards, start the game again!

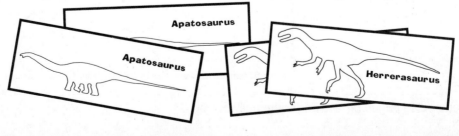

Math

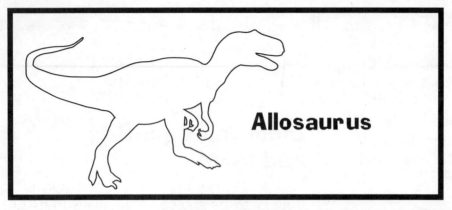

Allosaurus

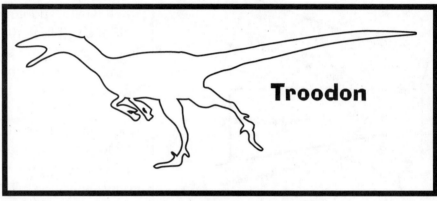

Troodon

Herrerasaurus

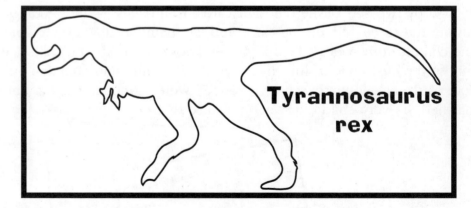

Tyrannosaurus rex

Teacher: Use pages 54 and 55 for the activities on 53.

Ankylosaurus

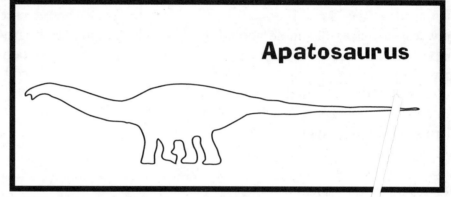

Apatosaurus

Stegosaurus

Triceratops

Math

Shaping Dinosaurs

Draw various sizes of simple geometric shapes (circles, squares, rectangles, triangles) on white construction paper. Photocopy the patterns, giving each child one sheet of geometric shapes. Let them cut out the shapes and arrange them to create a huge dinosaur! Have children glue their shape dinosaurs on construction paper. Encourage them to share their creatures, discussing the names of the shapes as they talk about their artwork. You may also ask other children to try and identify each shape used in the artwork.

Shapeosaurus

Cut out various sizes of simple geometric shapes (circles, squares, rectangles, triangles) from different colored construction paper. Let children help you create one huge "Shapeosaurus" on your wall. Help children develop their basic math skills by asking them questions such as: *How many big triangles in all? How many big blue triangles? How many big red triangles? Are there more big blue triangles or more big red triangles?* By focusing each day on a basic math skill, this bulletin board activity can be used again and again. Shapeosaurus might even become your class mascot!

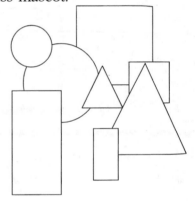

Dinosaur Shape Parade

Draw a set of small, simple geometric shapes (circles, squares, rectangles, triangles) on a strip of white paper. Photocopy the patterns, and give each child one pattern strip.
Let children cut out the shapes and glue them in any order on a long strip of construction paper. Then ask them to use markers and crayons to turn each shape into an imaginative dinosaur. Have them draw eyes, teeth, tails, claws, and other dinosaur details. Let children share their imaginative dinosaurs, inviting classmates to name each original geometric shape. Finally, display the artwork on a bulletin board titled "Dinosaur Shape Parade."

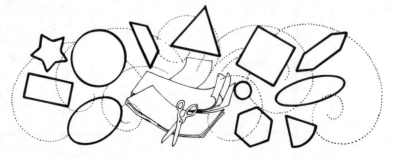

Sorting Spikes

Bring in a shoebox with a lid. Divide the inside of the lid into two sections. Attach a picture or sticker of a dinosaur with spikes or plates on one section of the lid, and a picture of a dinosaur without spikes on the other side. Then place a variety of plastic toy dinosaurs in the shoebox. Let children take turns sorting the toys into two groups by placing each dinosaur on its appropriate section of the lid.

Sorting Box

Place a collection of plastic toy dinosaurs in a box. Have children sit in a circle on the floor with the box in the middle. Each day, empty the box onto the floor and have children sort the dinosaurs in a different way. For example, have them begin by sorting the dinosaurs into pairs. The next day, have children sort the dinosaurs by size, length of tail, height, spikes/no spikes, and so on.

Comparing Characteristics

Place a variety of plastic toy dinosaurs in a shoebox. Invite a volunteer to pick out two dinosaurs and hold them up for the rest of the class to see. Ask children: *Which is the bigger dinosaur?* Let the child who answers correctly become the next child to choose two dinosaurs from the box. Repeat this activity by asking a series of different questions, such as: *Which dinosaur has the longer tail? Which dinosaur is taller? Which dinosaur is smaller?*

Math

One Leaf Per Dinosaur

Display pictures of plant-eating dinosaurs. (You could photocopy, color, and cut out the dinosaurs from pages 54 and 55, as well as dinosaurs such as Barosaurus, Corythosaurus, Edmontonia, Euoplocephalus, Hypsilophodon, Maiasaura, Parasaurolophus, and Styracosaurus.) Cut out large leaves from green construction paper and place them in a basket. Let children take turns pinning one leaf on each dinosaur. Repeat the activity, but this time display the leaves and let children pin a plant-eating dinosaur on each leaf. This simple activity reinforces one-to-one correspondence and also helps children recognize some of the plant-eating dinosaurs.

Dinosaur Tracks

Draw a simple dinosaur track with claws on a sheet of construction paper. Reproduce the track pattern to create 10 to 20 dinosaur footprints. Determine the sequence of numbers you want children to learn (*1–5, 1–10, 1–15*), and then print each number on a dinosaur track. Print the same sequence of numbers on a strip of paper and display it in the classroom. Mix up the numbered dinosaur tracks. Let children take turns ordering the numbers by laying the correct tracks in a line, using the number strip to guide them. After the numbers are ordered, let a child move from one print to the next, calling out the numbers as he or she goes.

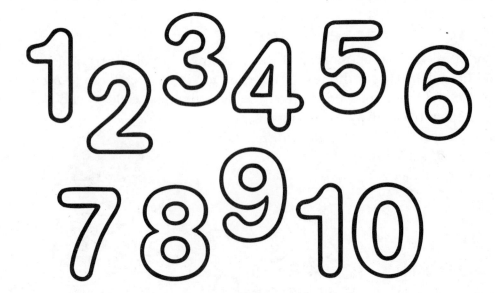

Sandbox Fun

Set out a large box filled with sand. Photocopy the dinosaurs from pages 54 and 55. Color and cut out the dinosaurs and attach them to individual craft sticks. Let children take turns placing the dinosaurs in the sand as you give directions such as the following: *Put a dinosaur in each corner of the box. Put three dinosaurs in the middle of the box. Put the dinosaurs side by side in three rows.* This fun activity fills those "extra minutes" at the end of the day and offers practice in spatial relationships.

 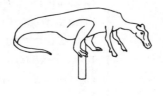 

Tracks in the Sand

Let children take off their shoes and socks. Then have them pretend to be dinosaurs roaming across the sandbox. Sand should be damp enough to hold footprints.
Demonstrate how to press down hard on the sand to leave clear impressions with hands and feet. Invite children to take turns walking upright or on "all fours" across the sandbox, leaving prints in the sand. Invite children to count how many prints were made. Rake over the prints and repeat the activity again and again!

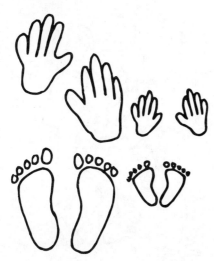

Following Directions

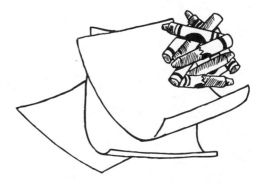

Buy multiple sets of dinosaur stickers so each child has four different dinosaurs. Give each child a crayon, four different dinosaur stickers, and a square of construction paper folded into fourths. Have children place one sticker inside each section. Then give them directions such as the following: *Put your finger on the sticker in the top right-hand corner of your paper. Draw a circle around that dinosaur. Put your finger on the sticker in the bottom left-hand corner. Draw a square around that dinosaur.* Continue giving similar directions as desired. Let children share their work with the class.

Math

Graphing Dinosaurs

Buy three sets of dinosaur stickers. Prepare a simple graph by drawing a grid on a large sheet of paper. Put a different dinosaur sticker in each square down the left side of the grid. Mount the rest of the stickers on individual index cards. Display the graph and set out the matching sticker cards. Let children take turns sorting the cards into separate piles of like dinosaurs. Have them count the number of dinosaurs in each pile. Ask them to find the matching dinosaur on the graph and color in one square for each additional dinosaur. Continue this process with the rest of the sticker cards.

What's Your Favorite Dinosaur?

Draw a simple outline for a bar graph on a long sheet of butcher paper. Put a different dinosaur sticker in each square down the left side of the grid. Write numerals across the bottom of the graph to show totals. Let children point to his or her favorite dinosaur. Have the children color one square in the row next to it, beginning with the first square on the left. After each child has colored a square, discuss the completed graph. Ask children: *Which dinosaur is most people's favorite? Which dinosaur got the least number of "votes"? Did any dinosaurs get the same number of votes?*

If You Were a Dinosaur...

Make signs by folding rectangular pieces of construction paper in half so they stand up. Put the same dinosaur sticker or picture on each side of the sign. (You may want to photocopy, color, and cut out the dinosaurs from pages 42, 43, 54, and 55.) Set out three signs, side by side. Have each child line up behind the sign that shows the dinosaur he or she would like to be! Then have the children in each line count off to reveal the total number who favored that dinosaur. Follow this same process to graph a different set of dinosaurs!

Measuring Dinosaurs

Before beginning this activity, cut 1" x 7" strips from slick magazine pages. Demonstrate how to glue together the ends of a strip to form a loop. Show how to make a chain by forming one paper strip at a time into a loop and gluing the ends together, one laced through another. Use a measuring tape to make the chain eight feet long. Attach a colorful self-stick note at each footmark. Let children use the paper chain to measure the width of one another's jaws. Have one child hold the end of the paper chain and extend it up three feet. Tell children that Tyrannosaurus rex had a jaw that was three feet wide. Next, let children measure one another's heights. Extend the chain up to six feet, telling children that Protoceratops was six feet long. Finally, let children measure the length of one another's heads. Extend the chain to its full length, and tell children that Pentaceratops had a head that was seven and a half feet long!

BIG Measurements

To prepare for this activity, mount pictures of different dinosaurs on separate sturdy paper plates. (See the list of dinosaurs and their lengths below.) Punch a hole at the top of each plate. Then measure and cut a section of yarn the length of each dinosaur. Tie one end of each yarn piece to the hole of the corresponding plate and lightly wrap the yarn around the plate. Take children outdoors, and let them take turns unwrapping the yarn for different dinosaurs to discover how big some dinosaurs really were! The following are approximate lengths.

    6 feet— Protoceratops
   15 feet— Camptosaurus, Ankylosaurus
   25 feet— Stegosaurus, Triceratops,
            Iguanodon
   50 feet— Tyrannosaurus rex
   85 feet— Apatosaurus, Brachiosaurus,
            Diplodocus
   90 feet— Diplodocus
  100 feet— Ultrasaurus

As a follow-up activity, have children use yardsticks, measuring tapes, and rulers to "measure" the lengths of other objects as well as themselves.

Music and Movement

Music and movement work together naturally for young children. These active experiences provide children with a fun way to express themselves while developing fine and gross motor skills, and showing what they've learned about dinosaurs.

Hatching Dinosaurs

Place hula hoops in an area that provides a lot of space for free movement. Have children form small groups and stand inside the hula hoops. Invite them to pretend to be dinosaur eggs in nests. Call out, "Hatch!" and have children jump outside the hula hoops. Call out, "Hide!" and have each child run and stand inside a different hula hoop. Repeat this activity until children have moved in and out of several different hula hoops.

Dinosaurs Lived Long Ago

Have children act out the words to this song as you sing it.

Dinosaurs Lived Long Ago
(Sung to the tune "Twinkle, Twinkle, Little Star")

Dinosaurs lived long ago,
Some moved fast and some moved slow.
Dinosaurs were big and small,
Some were short and some were tall.
Dinosaurs ate plants and meat,
Some were scary; some were neat!

Marsha Elyn Wright

Musical Dinosaurs

Tell children that no one really knows if dinosaurs made sounds. Scientists can only guess that dinosaurs made sounds by studying present-day animal behavior. Tell children to pretend they are dinosaurs. At your signal, have them move like dinosaurs, using musical instruments to make "dinosaur sounds." Let children trade instruments and repeat this simple game. See how many different sounds children can come up with!

Music and Movement

Yum, Yum, Food!

Have children sit in a large circle. Tell them to pretend they are plant-eating dinosaurs. Choose one child to be a meat-eater. Have the meat-eater walk around the outside of the circle, tapping each child lightly on the shoulder and calling out either "yum" or "food." If the meat-eater calls out "food," that plant-eater must chase the meat-eater around the outside of the circle and try to tag him or her before sitting in the plant-eater's spot. If tagged in time, the plant-eater becomes the next meat-eater. If not tagged in time, then the meat-eater chooses a new meat-eating dinosaur!

Catch 'em!

Place children in two groups—meat-eaters and plant-eaters. Use masking tape to mark a line at one end of the room and a second line at the other end. Have the plant-eaters wait behind the first line and the meat-eaters pretend to be asleep behind the other line. Tell the plant-eaters to slowly creep up to the meat-eaters. When you call out, "Catch 'em!" have the meat-eaters "wake up" and chase the plant-eaters, trying to tag them before they get back behind their line. Tagged plant-eaters join the meat-eaters. After all the plant-eaters are tagged, switch roles and play again.

Balance Beam Challenge

Set up a balance beam in your room. (You can make one by cutting a 4" x 12" paper strip and taping it to the floor.) Collect plastic flowers and leaves that children can easily pick up as they walk along the balance beam. Place the flowers and leaves within easy reach along the length of the beam. Then have children pretend to be hungry plant-eating dinosaurs. Invite them to walk across the balance beam, one at a time, and pick up a specific colored plant. Encourage children to pick up the plants without putting their feet on the floor and continue moving along the beam to the end. When a child reaches the end, collect the objects he or she picked up, so you can replace them next to the balance beam for the next "dinosaur."

Dinosaur Trap

Have children stand in two rows, facing each other. Have facing pairs hold hands and lift their arms high to form a bridge. Tell the first pair to pretend they are dinosaurs and run under the bridge. When they reach the end, show them how to hold hands and become part of the bridge again. Continue until children learn how to run under the bridge and reconstruct it on the other end. Then, teach this song. At the end of the first verse, have children lower their arms and trap whoever is inside! Sing the second verse while children move their arms from side to side. At the end of the second verse, let the "dinosaurs" continue running under the bridge.

Dinosaurs (Sung to the tune "London Bridge")

Dinosaurs go fast and slow,
Here they come! Here they go!
Dinosaurs go fast and slow,
Big dinosaurs!

Move the trap from side to side,
Side to side, side to side,
Move the trap from side to side,
Big dinosaurs!

Marsha Elyn Wright

Drawing to Music

Discuss the world of dinosaurs with children while listening to music. Display pictures of dinosaurs to stimulate the discussion. While the music plays, let children draw pictures of what they imagine prehistoric earth looked like. Encourage children to draw trees, rocks, and lakes in their pictures. Ask them to share their musically inspired artwork.

Music and Movement

Dinos in a Row

Arrange children in a circle so each child is facing the back of the child in front of him or her. Have children squeeze together and hold onto the shoulders of the children in front of them. Then tell them to pretend to be dinosaurs, moving as a group while acting out the words to this song:

Dinos in a Row
(Sung to the tune "The Wheels on the Bus")

Dinos in a row go fast and slow,
Fast and slow, fast and slow,
Dinos in a row go fast and slow,
All through the land.

Claws on their feet go scritch, scritch, scratch,
Scritch, scritch, scratch; scritch, scritch, scratch,
Claws on their feet go scritch, scritch, scratch,
All through the land.

Tails on their backs go swish, swish, swish,
Swish, swish, swish; swish, swish, swish,
Tails on their backs go swish, swish, swish,
All through the land.

Teeth in their jaws go chomp, chomp, chomp,
Chomp, chomp, chomp; chomp, chomp, chomp,
Teeth in their jaws go chomp, chomp, chomp,
All through the land.

Horns on their heads go honk, honk, honk,
Honk, honk, honk; honk, honk, honk,
Horns on their heads go honk, honk, honk,
All through the land.

Marsha Elyn Wright

Dinosaurs, Run!

Have children pretend they are going on a hike looking for dinosaurs. Invite them to march in place to a simple rhythm while counting *1, 2, 3,* and so on. At random times, call out, "Look out! Dinosaurs!" Tell children to run in place until you say, "Stop!" Repeat the activity several times. Children will love this active game!

I'm a Dinosaurus!

Have children pretend to be imaginary plant-eating dinosaurs named "Dinosaurus." Have them walk on all fours as they act out the words to this song:

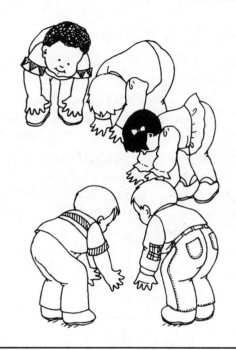

I'm a Dinosaurus!
(Sung to the tune "I'm a Little Teapot")

I'm a Dinosaurus, hear me wail,
Here is my duck bill, here is my tail.
Chomping on a big plant makes me leap,
And walk to my nest and go to sleep.

Marsha Elyn Wright

Be Brave, Dinosaurs

Remind children how plant-eating dinosaurs used their spiked tails, horns, and bodies to scare away meat-eating enemies. Let children pretend to be big, brave dinosaurs scaring away their enemies as they perform the motions to this song:

Be Brave, Dinosaurs
(Sung to the tune "Twinkle, Twinkle, Little Star")

Swing your big tail like a whip,
Quick and fast, run zip, zip, zip!
Poke your horns out,
Sound your call,
Move your spikes,
And stand real tall.
Scare away your enemies,
You are so brave,
just like me!

Marsha Elyn Wright

Dinosaur Walk

Set out carpet squares in rows of two to form a path. Remind children that some dinosaurs walked upright on two legs and some walked on all four legs. Play some lively music, and have children pretend to be dinosaurs. Tell them to walk upright along the path. When you stop the music, children will stop. When you start the music again, have them change from walking on two legs to four legs. Continue by stopping and starting the music until everyone has walked the path.

Music and Movement

Shadow Dinosaurs

Invite children to join you outdoors on a sunny afternoon. Have them stand in a circle so they can see one another's shadows. Encourage children to explore ways to make their shadows look like dinosaurs. Remind them that some dinosaurs walked upright on two legs and some walked on all fours. Suggest that children standing side by side can pair up to make one big dinosaur!

Dinosaur Cheers

Tell children to act as if they're in their own dinosaur fan club! Give each child a pompom or streamer. Teach them a simple routine to music as they spell the word *dinosaur* (*Give me a d!* D! *Give me an i!* I! and so on). Make sure children spread out so their movements don't hurt someone else. Once children learn how to spell *dinosaur*, try spelling other related words or dinosaur names.

Dinosaur Feet

Ask children to remove their shoes and socks. (Some children may want to wear their socks.) Take them outside and form a circle on the grass. Make sure the grass is free of litter so children don't get hurt stepping on broken plastic or glass. Tell children to pretend they are dinosaurs walking on the earth in prehistoric times. Have children walk around the circle, noting how the grass feels on their feet. Repeat this activity on sand, if possible. Stimulate a discussion by asking children questions such as: *What did the grass feel like? What did the sand feel like? Which did you like better? Which do you think dinosaurs would have liked better? Why? What are some surfaces that dinosaurs might not have liked?* (sharp rocks, mountains, steep hills)

Dinosaur Babies

Invite children on an outdoor walk. Tell them that Maiasaura was a dinosaur that built nests, laid eggs, and cared for its young babies. Tell children that *Maiasaura* means "good mother lizard." Have children pretend that you are the adult Maiasaura and they are your babies. Tell children to follow you and your actions as you walk around the playground. Vary how you move your arms, head, and legs during the walk. Encourage children to add imaginative tiny dinosaur sounds like babies might have made. To add excitement, call out, "Run! Enemies!" At the warning, have children move very quickly as they follow you, until you call out, "Stop! Whew! We're safe!"

Tyrannosaurus rex Tag

Take children outdoors for this unique game of tag. Choose some children to be trees. Have the "trees" hold up their arms and sway in the breeze. Choose one child to be a Tyrannosaurus rex, a meat-eating dinosaur. Have the other children be plant-eating dinosaurs. Tell the Tyrannosaurus rex to stand by the trees. Have the plant-eaters stand in a line about ten feet away. At your signal, the plant-eaters try to run to one of the trees without getting tagged by the Tyrannosaurus rex. If a plant-eater is tagged before reaching a tree, the plant-eater becomes a Tyrannosaurus rex as well. The two meat-eaters then join hands as they try to tag the rest of the plant-eaters. Start the game again by telling all the Tyrannosaurus rexes to join hands in one long line as they move around trying to tag plant-eaters. Play until the last plant-eater is tagged. When you play this again, make sure children who were trees get a chance to be dinosaurs.

Music and Movement

Prehistoric Rain Showers

Let each child put a handful of small items, such as uncooked rice, dried beans, or dried peas, inside a small box, an egg carton, or an oatmeal container. Securely seal each container with tape. Let children decorate their containers 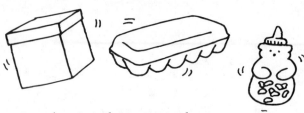 with stickers and paper streamers. Tell them to imagine that it is long ago when there are only huge dinosaurs (no people) roaming the earth. It is filled with tall trees, ferns, oceans, rocks, lakes, and volcanoes. Invite children to use their shakers to create a "rain shower" for this prehistoric setting. If possible, play soft music in the background and turn off the lights. Have children sit in a circle, holding their shakers. Start moving your shaker softly and slowly. Invite the child sitting next to you to join in your rhythm with his or her shaker. Keep pointing to each child, gradually speeding up your rhythm, so the rain shower gets louder and louder. Begin slowing down your shaker, getting softer and softer until you stop. Try it again, randomly pointing to different children. You can create a soft rain shower or a fierce storm!

Hatching from Eggs

Invite children to pretend they are baby dinosaurs hatching from eggs. Teach them the motions to this song, and have them sing along as they act out the words.

I'm Inside an Egg
(Sung to the tune "Turkey in the Straw")

I'm inside an egg,
   (Lay on your back. Crouch into a ball.)
And I wobble to and fro.
   (Rock back and forth.)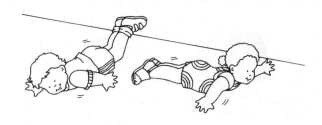
Can you hear me tap?
   (Tap the floor with fingers.)
Can you hear me grow?
   (Push arms and legs outward.)
Can you hear the eggshell cracking as I'm tapping one, two, three?
   (Hold up one, two, and then three fingers.)
Look at me! I'm free!
   (Jump up and run away.)

Marsha Elyn Wright

Dinosaur Hokey-Pokey

Invite children to act like dinosaurs as they sing and act out this song:

Dinosaur Hokey-Pokey
(Sung to the tune "The Hokey-Pokey")

I put my right claw in,
I pull my right claw out,
I put my right claw in, and I shake it all about.
I do the hokey-pokey and I stomp all around,
That's what it's all about!

I put my left claw in,
I pull my left claw out,
I put my left claw in, and I shake it all about.
I do the hokey-pokey and I stomp all around,
That's what it's all about!

Marsha Elyn Wright

Verse #3: I put my right foot in . . .
Verse #4: I put my left foot in . . .
Verse #5: I put my long neck in . . .
Verse #6: I put my spiked tail in . . .
Verse #7: I put my whole self in . .

Chant with the Beat

Sit in a circle with children, and place a drum in front of you. Help children learn common dinosaur names by chanting them with the drum. Chant a dinosaur name (*Allosaurus, Ankylosaurus, Apatosaurus, Diplodocus, Iguanodon, Stegosaurus, Triceratops, Tyrannosaurus rex*). Tap out the name on the drum as you chant, accenting the main syllable with a stronger drumbeat. Invite children to chant along with you!

Music and Movement

Dinosaurs—Honk! Honk!

Tell children that scientists believe some dinosaurs with crests on their heads made loud honking sounds or long sounds like a hunting horn. The Saurolophus and Parasaurolophus were two of these crested dinosaurs. Cover one end of a paper towel tube with waxed paper, securing the paper with a rubber band. Let children pretend they are bone-crested dinosaurs honking "hello" to each other! Demonstrate how to hum into the open end of a tube to make a horn-like sound. Encourage children to explore making other "dinosaur noises" with their tubes.

Young Dinosaurs at Play

Have children act like young dinosaurs at play. First, pair up children. Designate one partner from each pair as the leader. Then have each leader move around like a dinosaur while his or her partner tries to copy the movements, as if looking in a mirror. Play lively music in the background to encourage lots of movement. Stop the music so partners can switch roles and play again.

Swing and Sway

Invite children to create a prehistoric setting using scarves, crepe paper streamers, and blankets. Have children bunch up the blankets to make "boulders" and "hills." Select some children to be trees, swinging and swaying their branches (streamers) in the wind. Choose some children to be flying prehistoric reptiles that move their wings (scarves) up and down as they fly. Let the rest of the children be land-roaming dinosaurs. Play lively music in the background to signal children to begin moving. When you stop the music, tell them to freeze. Once the music begins again, children resume their movements. Repeat this activity several times, letting children switch roles.

Parent Involvement

Invite parents to join in the fun with these lively activities. They will promote parent interaction, maintaining an open, two-way communication between home and school.

Parent Involvement

Dinosaur Day

Host a Dinosaur Day, inviting each child to be an imaginary dinosaur for the day! Help each child print his or her name with the suffix –*osaurus* on a large dinosaur-shaped nametag (*Clayosaurus*). Send home a letter announcing Dinosaur Day. Ask parents to help their children practice pronouncing their dinosaur names. Also, ask parents to print words that their children dictate to them, describing what they look like (*long tail, spikes, plates, big horns*). Have parents print each word on the nametags. If possible, make dinosaur-shaped cookies, and invite parents to join the day at a specified time. During that time, read fun, fascinating dinosaur books such as *If the Dinosaurs Came Back* by Bernard Most (Harcourt Brace & Co., 1978), *The Smallest Stegosaurus* by Lynn Sweat and Louis Phillips (Puffin, 1995), and *Can I Have a Stegosaurus, Mom? Can I? Please!?* by Lois G. Grambling (Troll Associates, 1998). You may even want to have a craft time in which children and parents can make paper-plate dinosaur masks. Have children wear their masks and take turns describing the kinds of dinosaurs they are. Wrap up your special day with a dinosaur parade!

Dictating Dinosaur Stories

Make a blank book with a construction paper cover for each child. Have children draw pictures of dinosaurs and tell you stories about their pictures. For each child, print the words to the stories underneath the pictures. Leave blank pages at the back of each book. Then send the books home with a parent letter. In each letter, explain that the class has been working on telling and drawing dinosaur stories. Share how you wrote down the words as the child dictated the story to you. Ask parents to read the story, and then have their child draw and dictate another dinosaur picture story that they can write out. Encourage parents to jot down comments about their learning experiences with their children. Tell parents that you will share the new stories with all the children in class when the books are returned.

"Cooperative Dig" Parent Letter

_____
(date)

Dear Parent(s),

We would love to have your help in setting up a "Dinosaur Dig" on _____. If you are interested, please check the areas below with which you can assist, and send the list back to school with your child. Thank you for your help!

Sincerely,

_____

Name: _____

Phone Numbers: Work _____ Home _____

_____ 1. **Parent Paleontologists** (assist children with digging for fossils; ask children questions about what they found)

_____ 2. **Tool Managers** (collect and hand out plastic spoons and old, clean toothbrushes)

_____ 3. **Sand Managers** (collect and fill baking pans or dish pans with sand; empty pans into sandbox when activity is over)

_____ 4. **Snack Chefs** (bring paper cups and napkins; make Dinosaur Trail Mix with pretzels, assorted nuts, raisins, chocolate bits, and granola cereal; donate and distribute fruit juice)

_____
(date)

Dear Parent(s),

Thank you for helping with our "Dinosaur Dig"! Please bring your materials or foodstuffs to our room by _____. On the day of the dig, come to our room by _____. See you then!

Thank you,

_____

Teacher: Use this parent letter for "Cooperative Dig" on page 75.

Parent Involvement

Habitat Hunt

Create one art bag for each child. Each self-sealing bag will contain a roll of construction paper, dinosaur cutouts, scissors, and glue. Title a bulletin board "Habitat Hunt," and send home the parent letter (page 79) to explain the activity. The letter invites parents to help their children collect nature items—twigs, grass clippings, leaves, and bark. Ask children to take home the art bags and create pictures of prehistoric habitats using their collected nature items and dinosaur cutouts. When children return their artwork and art bags, let them take turns presenting their creations. Display all of children's artwork on the "Habitat Hunt" bulletin board. Read aloud any parent comments to the class.

Stegosaurus Sandwiches

Invite parents into the classroom to help you prepare Stegosaurus sandwiches! Ask them to prepare a paper plate for each child. On each plate, place five slices of cheese cut into small triangular shapes, one half circle of bread, four carrot sticks, two celery sticks (one short and one long), and a spoonful of peanut butter. Have children form small groups. Then ask parent volunteers to give each child a prepared paper plate. Have parents help children follow these directions: Spread peanut butter on the bread to make the Stegosaurus body. Arrange four carrots sticks below the body for legs. Place the short piece of celery on an angle for the neck and the long celery piece at the back of the body for the tail. Add triangular pieces of cheese along the Stegosaurus's back for dinosaur plates. Finally, add a cheese triangle on top of the neck as a head. Invite parents to make dinosaur treats for themselves as well. Have everyone enjoy their treats while you read a book about dinosaurs! (See page 45 for a book list.)

Measuring Bones

Wash and air-dry a variety of chicken, beef, and pork bones. Place a set of bones and a ruler in separate self-sealing plastic bags. Tell children that scientists use rulers to measure dinosaur bones. Explain that they will each take home a measuring kit and measure bones with their parents' help. Send home a kit with the parent letter (page 79). After children return the kits and results to school, have each child share his or her measurements. Read any parent comments about this exciting learning experience.

"Habitat Hunt"
Parent Letter

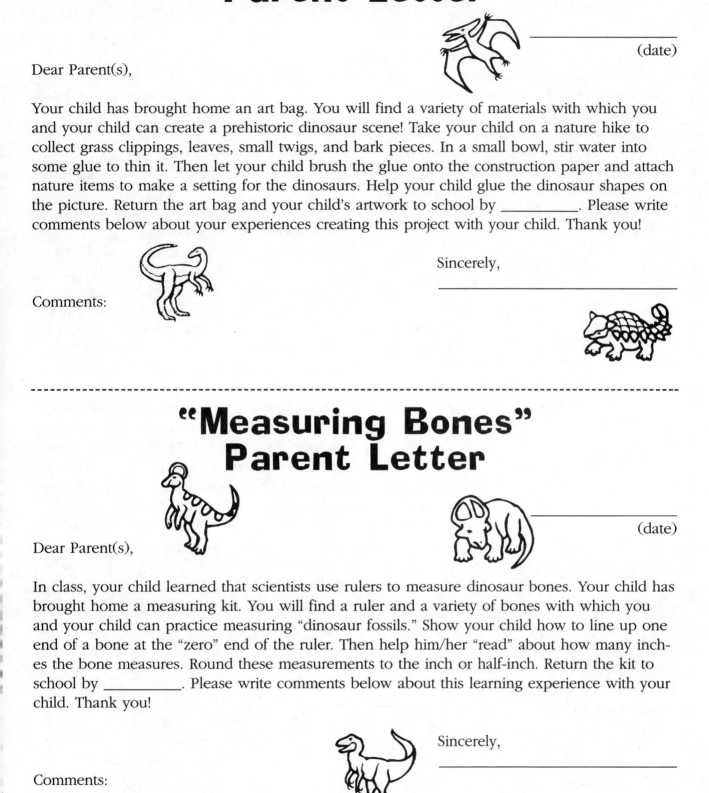

_____
(date)

Dear Parent(s),

Your child has brought home an art bag. You will find a variety of materials with which you and your child can create a prehistoric dinosaur scene! Take your child on a nature hike to collect grass clippings, leaves, small twigs, and bark pieces. In a small bowl, stir water into some glue to thin it. Then let your child brush the glue onto the construction paper and attach nature items to make a setting for the dinosaurs. Help your child glue the dinosaur shapes on the picture. Return the art bag and your child's artwork to school by _____. Please write comments below about your experiences creating this project with your child. Thank you!

Sincerely,

_____

Comments:

"Measuring Bones"
Parent Letter

_____
(date)

Dear Parent(s),

In class, your child learned that scientists use rulers to measure dinosaur bones. Your child has brought home a measuring kit. You will find a ruler and a variety of bones with which you and your child can practice measuring "dinosaur fossils." Show your child how to line up one end of a bone at the "zero" end of the ruler. Then help him/her "read" about how many inches the bone measures. Round these measurements to the inch or half-inch. Return the kit to school by _____. Please write comments below about this learning experience with your child. Thank you!

Sincerely,

_____

Comments:

Teacher: Use these parent letters for the activities on page 78.

1-57029-483-6 _Theme-a-Saurus: Dinosaurs_

Parent Involvement

"Nest of Eggs" Toss

Place a piece of fabric, a plastic bowl, and a set of plastic eggs inside separate plastic storage containers with handles. (Prepare about four containers.) Within each container, place the parent letter and directions for the "Nest of Eggs" Toss (page 81). Let children take turns bringing home the game containers and playing "Nest of Eggs" Toss with their families. Invite children to share their experiences with the class.

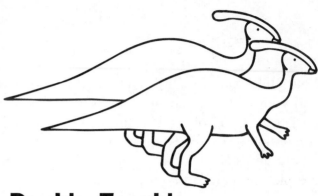

Double Trouble

Buy multiple sets of dinosaur stickers. Place the stickers on separate index cards to create duplicate sets of dinosaur sticker cards. Put a duplicate set of cards inside a self-sealing plastic bag to make one "Double Trouble" game. Demonstrate how to play Double Trouble following these directions: Mix up the dinosaur cards. Lay them facedown in three rows. The first player turns over two cards. If the dinosaurs match, the player gets to keep the cards. If the dinosaurs don't match, the player returns the cards, facedown, in their original spots. Then the next player takes a turn. Play continues until all the cards are matched. Make several game bags, so children can take turns bringing home the bags and playing Double Trouble with their families.

Footprint Fun

Cut out multiple sets of dinosaur footprints from construction paper. Make a set of small prints, medium-sized prints, and large prints. Place the "Footprint Fun" parent letter and game instructions (page 81), and about five of each size footprints inside a self-sealing plastic bag. Invite children to take home the bags to play this fun counting game with their families.

"Nest of Eggs" Toss
Parent Letter

Dear Parent(s),

_____
(date)

Your child has brought home a game bag to play "Nest of Eggs" Toss. Please play this fun game with your child. Teach him/her the following game directions:

Place the fabric inside the bowl to make a dinosaur nest. Stand about two feet away from the nest, and try to toss as many eggs into the bowl as you can without bouncing them out. Count the eggs in the bowl. Let the next player take a turn. Whoever tosses the most eggs into the nest wins the round. Play again and again! Return the game bag to school by _____. Write comments below describing your experiences playing this game with your child.

Comments:

Thank you,

_____

"Footprint Fun"
Parent Letter

Dear Parent(s),

_____
(date)

Your child has brought home a game bag to play "Footprint Fun." Please play this fun game with your child. First, lay out the dinosaur footprints randomly in rows. Then help your child answer the following questions:

- How many small footprints are there? Count them.
- How many big footprints are there? Count them.
- Are there more small footprints or big footprints?
- How many medium-sized footprints are there?
- Make a path of footprints. How many footprints are there in all?
- Can you count all the footprints in the bag? Try it!

Return the game bag to school by _____. Write comments below about your experiences playing this game with your child. Thank you!

Comments:

Sincerely,

_____

Teacher: Use these parent letters for the activities on page 80.

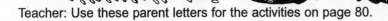

Science

The following activities involve children in concrete, hands-on experiences that include familiar materials and concepts from the physical world. Invite children to join you on an exploration of the natural, scientific world of prehistoric times and creatures.

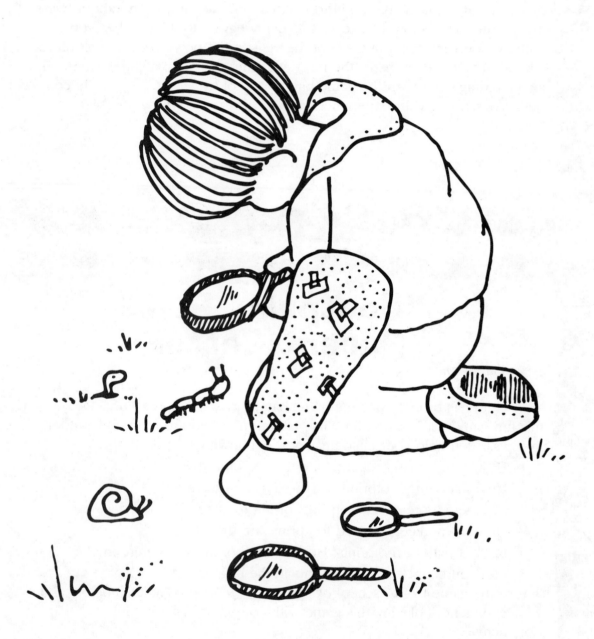

Living or Extinct?

Introduce children to the world of dinosaurs by teaching them the difference between living and extinct animals. Buy a variety of toy dinosaurs, and have each child bring a toy or stuffed animal to school. Place the stuffed animals and dinosaurs in a box, and ask children to sit in a circle around you. Place two stand-up signs—*Living* and *Extinct*—in the center of the circle. Tell children that dinosaurs lived on land long ago and are no longer living. Hold up several toy dinosaurs, and let children talk about them. Familiarize children with the word *extinct*. Hold up a toy dinosaur and another stuffed animal. Ask children:
Which animal is living today? Which animal is extinct?
Choose a child to put each animal behind the correct sign. Help children categorize the rest of the animals, lining up each toy behind *Living* or *Extinct*.

Eggs in a Nest

Prepare for this activity by gathering several plastic eggs. Make a "dinosaur nest" out of sand in a plastic dishpan. Tell children that many mother dinosaurs dug a nest for their eggs in the earth. If possible, show children a picture of a Maiasaura. Maiasaura mothers dug bowl-shaped nests for their eggs in the earth. Display the nest and put some of the eggs inside of it. Ask children to guess how many eggs they think are in the nest. Record their guesses. Let children count together as you hold up each egg to see how close their estimates were to the actual number. Repeat this activity each day, changing the number of eggs each time.

Building Habitats

At a center, set out a dish pan of wet sand, plastic toy dinosaurs, rocks, and plastic plants. Let children take turns arranging the rocks, trees, and dinosaurs into a prehistoric habitat. After each child creates a habitat, have him or her share it with the class. Take a photograph of each child next to his or her habitat. Display the photographs on a bulletin board titled "Building Habitats."

Science

How Did They Walk?

Collect a variety of pictures showing dinosaurs that walked on all four legs and dinosaurs that walked upright on two hind legs. Mount each picture on construction paper. Mix up the pictures and place them facedown in front of the class. Remind children that some dinosaurs walked on all four legs and some walked upright on two back legs. Then turn over a dinosaur picture. Ask children: *Did this dinosaur walk on all four legs or did it walk on two hind legs?* Place each picture in a separate pile. Let children take turns drawing pictures from the top of the pile and sorting the dinosaurs by how they walked.

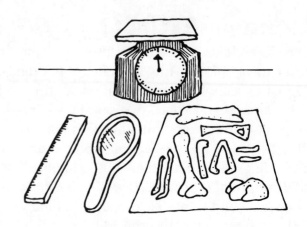

Bone Exploration

Clean and air-dry a variety of pork, beef, and chicken bones. Show children the bones. Help them compare bones by asking some of the following questions: *Which bone is longer? Which bone is thicker? Which bone is heavier? How are the bones different? How are the bones alike?*
Tell children that scientists have learned about dinosaurs by studying the remains of their bones. They call these old bones "fossils." Set out a ruler, magnifying glass, and a scale. Let children use the items to weigh, measure, and study the bones.

Prehistoric Animals

Collect a variety of pictures of prehistoric animals that lived on land, flew in the air, or lived in the water. Tell children that dinosaurs lived only on land, but other prehistoric animals lived in the water and flew in the air. Cut out three large circles from brown, blue, and white construction paper. Gather children in a circle, and place the circles in the center. Display the animal pictures. Let children take turns choosing an animal picture and placing it on the brown circle if the animal lived on land, the blue circle if it lived in the water, or the white circle if it could fly.

Grabbing for Grub

Collect a variety of plastic foods, including meats and vegetables. Place these items in a drawstring bag (or pillowcase with a rubber band). Remind children that some dinosaurs ate meat and some ate plants. Explain how meat-eaters had sharp, pointed teeth for tearing the meat, and plant-eaters had flat teeth for grinding the plants. Let children pretend they are dinosaurs. Show them the bag of "food." One at a time, have children tell you if he or she is a meat-eater or plant-eater. Invite the child to put his or her hand inside the bag and pull out a food item. If the food is appropriate, have the child sit down with the item. If the food is not appropriate, have the child return the food to the bag and sit down. After each child has had a turn, let the "hungry dinosaurs" try grabbing for grub until they get the right kind of food!

Tools of the Trade

Clean and air-dry a variety of pork, beef, and chicken bones. Collect several tape measures, small hammers, wide paintbrushes, and small pieces of burlap. Bury the bones in a large box filled with sand. Tell children that scientists who study dinosaurs from long ago are called "paleontologists." Explain that these scientists use special tools to dig up and study the remains of dinosaur bones, called "fossils." Hold up each tool and tell children its use:

Tape measure: used to measure the size of fossils
Hammer: used to dig out tiny amounts of rock
Brush: used to gently sweep away sand and dust from fossils
Burlap: used to wrap up fossils so they
   won't break

Set out the box of buried "fossils" and the tools. Let children take turns digging for the bones and wrapping up their discoveries in burlap. Let each child share what he or she discovered!

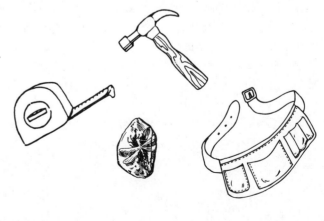

Science

Making Fossils

Make gray modeling clay by adding black tempera paint to any color of modeling clay. Place the gray clay in a plastic container with a lid. Set out a tagboard work mat, paper towels (for wiping hands), and toy plastic dinosaurs. Have children take turns grab-bing a ball of clay, flattening it  out on the work mat, and pressing a plastic dinosaur into the smooth surface. Demonstrate how to carefully remove the dinosaur to see the imprint left behind in the clay. Tell children that these impressions are similar to the fossils left by real dinosaurs millions of years ago under layers of sand and mud in the earth. Let each child tell about his or her dinosaur fossil. Use a craft stick to print each child's name on his or her fossil and set it out to dry. After dis-playing the fossils, let children take them home to share with their families.

Prehistoric Eruptions

Prepare several containers or tubs of wet sand. Place the sand tubs on newspaper. Set out containers of baking soda, plastic cups, and plastic spoons. Then have children form small groups, and assign each group a sand tub. Explain to children that during the days of the dinosaurs there were many active volcanoes on the earth. Invite each group to work together to mold a volcano out of the wet sand in the tub. (You may want to provide children with pictures of volcanoes to use as references.) Help each group hollow out the middle of its volcano so a plastic cup will fit in the hole. Then place two spoonfuls of baking soda in each plastic cup. Let children take turns placing a plastic cup in the middle of their volcanoes. Walk around the room, pouring a quarter cup of vinegar into each cup. Tell children that baking soda and vinegar mix together to make a gas, which pushes its way out of the cup. Explain that this action is similar to the gases in an active volcano, pushing up hot, liquid rock. Children will love watching their volcanoes react with foamy eruptions!

Clawed Feet

Tell children that meat-eating dinosaurs had huge curved claws on their feet, and they used these claws to protect themselves and to eat. Tape three small craft sticks on the fingers of each child's right hand. First, wrap tape around the child's thumb and a craft stick. Next, have the child hold his or her index finger and middle finger together while you wrap tape around them, along with a craft stick. Have the child hold his or her ring finger and little finger together; wrap tape around these fingers, along with another craft stick. Tell children to pretend that these are their dinosaur claws. Challenge them to use their "claws" to eat chicken strips. Encourage children to explore different ways to grab the food with their craft-stick claws. Then let them remove their claws and enjoy their snacks!

Plant-Eater or Meat-Eater?

Reproduce multiple copies of the dinosaur cards on pages 54 and 55. Glue one meat-eater (Allosaurus, Herrerasaurus, Troodon, or Tyrannosaurus rex) and one plant-eater (Ankylosaurus, Apatosaurus, Stegosaurus, or Triceratops) on separate Styrofoam meat trays. Draw a chicken leg (drumstick) on the tray showing the meat-eater, and a tree on the tray showing the plant-eater. Mix up and stack the rest of the dinosaur cards. Explain to children that some dinosaurs ate only meat and some ate only plants. Let children take turns sorting the dinosaurs into the two groups by placing the cards in the corresponding trays.

Science

Trapped in Tar

Tell children that at the time of the dinosaurs large puddles of thick, black liquid called tar formed on the earth. Explain that tar is made from coal or wood. Dinosaurs often got stuck and died in these large tar pits. Scientists often find dinosaur fossils in tar pits. Fill a dishpan with water, red and blue food coloring, and liquid bubble bath to make a "tar pit." (You can also heat a mixture of water, food coloring, and gelatin, and then pour the thick liquid into a dishpan. Make sure the mixture cools before children use it.) At a center, place the dishpan on a large towel, and set out a variety of plastic toy dinosaurs. Invite children to take turns "trapping" the dinosaurs in the tar. Encourage them to make the dinosaurs "talk" to one another. Let each child have an opportunity to share his or her experience.

The Watering Hole

Tell children that many dinosaurs walked through shallow lakes to feed on water plants, get drinks, and cool themselves. Pour a layer of sand in a shallow tub, and add a few inches of water. Set out the tub, some toy dinosaurs, and a container of small items such as corks for floating "driftwood," plastic leaves, rocks, and shells. Let children take turns creating a water environment for the dinosaurs. Encourage them to make the dinosaurs swim, drink, and play in the water.

Dinosaur Names

Use several sets of magnetic letters and magnetic boards to help children learn the names of different dinosaurs. Mount pictures of "popular" or well-known dinosaurs (Tyrannosaurus rex, Stegosaurus, Triceratops, Apatosaurus, Iguanodon) on separate pieces of tagboard. Print the name of each dinosaur below its picture. Cover the cards with clear self-stick paper for durability. Attach a strip of magnetic tape to the back of each card. Then give each child a dinosaur card. Invite him or her to use the magnetic letters and board to copy the name printed on the card.

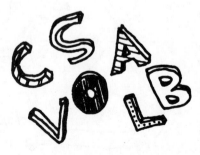

These engaging ideas involve young children in cooperative activities that inspire the spirit of cooperation and working together. Children will learn about dinosaurs as well as discover more about themselves!

Social Studies

Survey the School

Make simple recording forms for children to use for conducting their own surveys. At the top of each form, write the question: *Which is your favorite dinosaur?* On the left-hand side of the form, below the question, attach a column of dinosaur stickers. Draw a grid to separate the stickers and to provide a place where children can tally responses to the question. Put the forms on clipboards and hand them out. Tell your class to interview children in other classes or their families. They will record answers to the survey question by making tally marks next to the pictures on their forms. After the survey is completed, let children share their results. Ask questions such as: *Which dinosaur is the most popular? Why do you think it is so popular? Which dinosaur is the least popular? Why? Are any two dinosaurs liked equally well?*

Our BIG BOOK Dinosaur Story

Use a pad of chart paper to write a cooperative class book about dinosaurs. Invite children to spend time talking about what they have learned about dinosaurs. Then encourage them to make up a dinosaur story! Have one child at a time dictate a sentence to you as you write it at the bottom of a sheet of chart paper. Print the name of the child by his or her sentence. Read back each sentence as the story progresses to help children continue the plot. After each child takes a turn, read back the story, pointing to each word as you go. Add an ending, if needed. Number the pages and distribute each page to its author. Let children illustrate their sentences, and then bind the pages together into a BIG BOOK Dinosaur Story! Add a cover and let children sign their names. Host a "Story Day," and invite another class to listen to children as they read from their big book.

Cooperative Voting

Display long strips of butcher paper. While studying dinosaurs, print each dinosaur-related word children learn. Each day, review the words on the list. You may want to set out paper strips, crayons, and pencils for children to create their own dinosaur word lists. Encourage children to draw or "write" any words they learn. Let children share their lists with the class. Place children in small cooperative groups. Challenge each group to choose one word from all the lists as the group's favorite dinosaur word. Give children time to discuss their choices and then vote. Let each group share its favorite word and tell what it means. As a follow-up, talk with children about getting along within a group (how to behave when the group is doing something they don't like; how to behave when they want to talk to the group and no one is listening).

Group Sorting— DINO Bones

Clean and air-dry several different kinds (sizes and shapes) of beef, chicken, and pork bones. Place children in small cooperative groups. Give each group two large paper circles, a scale, a ruler, a magnifying glass, and a set of bones. Tell each group to lay their circles side by side to use as recording sheets. Explain that it is each group's goal to study the bones and sort them into two groups—long/short, heavy/light, bumpy/smooth—by placing the bones on the circles. Tell groups that it's up to them to decide how to sort the bones. After a group has sorted its bones, invite group members to share their results with the class.

Social Studies

Dinosaur Families

Tell children that scientists make guesses about how dinosaurs behaved by studying dinosaur fossils as well as present-day animal behavior. Explain that scientists believe many mother dinosaurs worked hard to dig dirt nests for their eggs and fought hard to protect their eggs and babies. Ask children how their parents' behavior is similar to how dinosaurs behaved. Discuss how parents provide "nests" for their families, as well as the ways parents protect their families. Then play soft music, and invite children to draw pictures of parents taking care of their families.

Dinosaur Video Party!

Videotape each child saying something he or she has learned about dinosaurs. Ask children to show their artwork on camera, and then sing the following dinosaur song with you. Play the tape back for the class to enjoy. You may even want to invite parents to your classroom to enjoy dinosaur-shaped cookies while they watch their children's videotaped performances on dinosaurs!

Dinosaurs Are Fun!
(Sung to the tune "Twinkle, Twinkle, Little Star")

Dinosaurs are fun for me,
Some eat plants and some eat trees,
Some have horns and some have claws,
Some have sharp teeth in their jaws.
Dinosaurs are big and small,
Dinosaurs are fun for all!

Marsha Elyn Wright

Dinosaur Pencil Toppers

Teacher: Photocopy these dinosaur pencil toppers, and give one to each child. Let children cut and color the dinosaurs. Punch the two holes in each topper, as shown. Demonstrate how to insert a pencil through the holes so the dinosaur stands up at the end of the pencil.

Dinosaur Bookmarks

Teacher: Photocopy the bookmarks, and give one to each child. Let children cut and color the bookmarks and use them in their favorite books!

94

1-57029-483-6 *Theme-a-Saurus: Dinosaurs*

Dinosaur Badges

King of Learners

DINO-MITE Learner

Super Scientist

Super Learn-a-saurus

Teacher: Photocopy these badges, and give one to each child. Let children cut and color the badges. Punch a hole in each badge, as shown, and tie a length of yarn through the hole to fit around a child's neck. Children will proudly wear these awards around their necks!

1-57029-483-6 *Theme-a-Saurus: Dinosaurs*

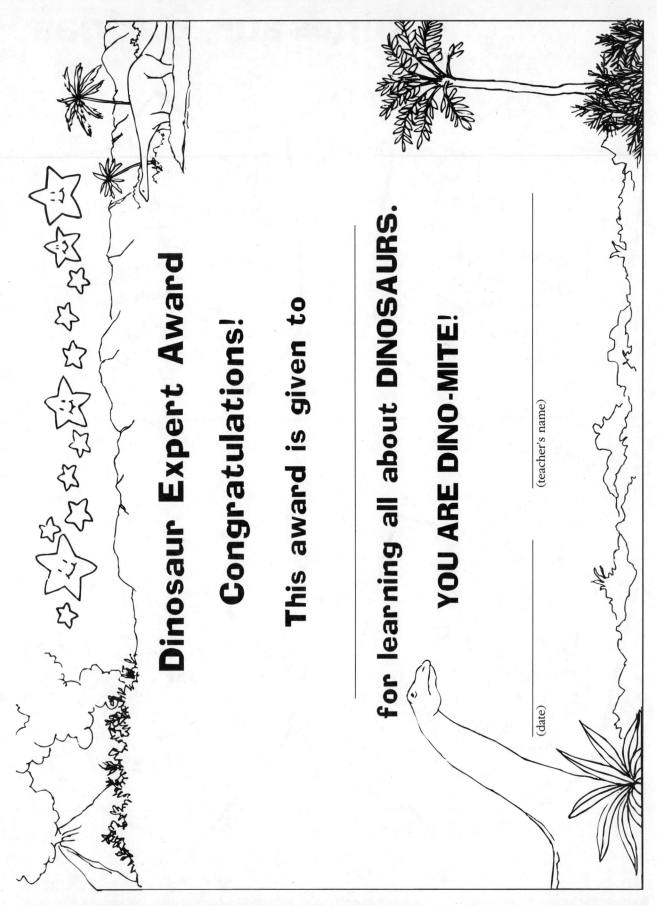

Dinosaur Expert Award

Congratulations!

This award is given to

_____

for learning all about DINOSAURS.

YOU ARE DINO-MITE!

_____
(teacher's name)

_____
(date)

Teacher: Photocopy this award, and present one to each child at the end of your dinosaur study. Let children color the awards and take them home to share with their families.